For the People

A Citizenship ESOL Text

Allene Grognet, Deborah Short, Margaret Seufert

DELTA PUBLISHING COMPANY
A Division of
DELTA SYSTEMS CO., INC.

Interior Design/Production: Linda Bruell
Cover: Damon Taylor

ISBN: 978–1–934960–14–1

10 9 8 7 6 5 4 3 2 1
First Edition

Printed in the United States of America

TABLE OF CONTENTS

TO THE STUDENT

We wrote this book for you. We hope you will think the lessons are interesting. We hope you will enjoy learning about U.S. government, history, and geography. The lessons can help you become better residents and citizens of the U.S.

Each lesson has a title. It tells you the subject of each lesson. Under each title there will be one or more objectives. These objectives say what you will learn from the lesson.

You will practice all your English skills—listening, speaking, reading, and writing. Most of the lessons have four parts:

I. Pre–Reading

II. Information

III. Reading

IV. Review

I. PRE–READING

In the first part of every lesson, **Pre–Reading**, you will find some questions to discuss with a partner, in a small group, or with the class. These questions will be about pictures, a map, or ideas about history or government.

After the discussion or map, you will find new vocabulary words. Their definitions will help you understand the lesson. Some of the words have other definitions, too. Sometimes you will have a written exercise to do.

Some exercises will tell you to guess. Guessing means you do not really know the answers. You give your ideas about what you think the answer will be.

Other exercises will tell you to scan a paragraph. When you scan, you do not read everything. You look for specific information to answer the questions.

II. Information

The **Information** is always on a chart, map, timeline, or in a diagram. It shows you the main points of the lesson.

First, think about the title. Next, read the information on the page carefully. Ask yourself questions about the information. For example:

- Who were the first settlers?

- Why did they come to the U.S.?

- Where did they settle?

- Who is the president?

- What does the president do?

- Where does the president live?

Finally, do the exercises—**Using the Information**. Look at the Information page to help you complete the speaking, listening, and writing exercises.

III. Reading

The **Reading** is usually one to five paragraphs long. Sometimes the **Reading** will give you more information about the main points. Sometimes the **Reading** will give you new information.

- First, think about the title.

- Next, read the paragraphs quickly for a general idea.

- Then, read the paragraphs carefully.

- Finally, do the exercise(s)—**Using the Reading**. Look at the **Reading** to help you complete the exercise(s).

IV. Review

These are the same questions that a USCIS officer will ask you. Many of the questions have more than <u>one</u> answer. If you are asked for one answer, choose from the answers and give only <u>one</u>. Here are some questions that want one answer:

- What is <u>one</u> right or freedom from the First Ammendment?

- Name <u>one</u> war fought by the U.S. in the 1800s.

- Name <u>one</u> of the longest rivers in the U.S.

Sometimes the USCIS officer will ask for two answers. Give only two answers. All of the answers to USCIS questions appear in **Bold** in the chapter you just studied. If you cannot answer the review questions, you should look back at the **Information** and **Reading** again. If you can answer the review questions, you can go to the next lesson.

What should you do if you are not in a class? What should you do if you are studying alone? If you are studying alone, show the lessons to your friends, or someone in your family, or someone at work. Ask people to help you practice your English. Ask them to be your partner for the speaking exercises. Ask them to do the group discussions with you.

Can you use this book if you **were not** born in the U.S.? **YES!**

Can you use this book if you **were** born in the U.S.? **YES!**

This book will help everyone learn more about U.S. history and government. Sometimes you will see questions about "your" country. If you were born in the U.S., answer these questions with information about the native country of your family or friends. You can also answer these questions with information about other countries you know.

ACKNOWLEDGMENTS

For the People: A Citizenship ESOL Text is an updated version of two books:
Of the People: U.S. History and **By the People, For the People: U.S. Governement and Citizenship** by Deborah J. Short, Margaret Seufert–Bosco, and Allene Guss Grognet. These books were published in 1991 and 1992 by the Center for Applied Linguistics and Delta Publishing Company.

In reviewing these two books to consolidate them and to bring them in line with the new U.S. Citizenship and Immigration Services guidelines and test for citizenship, I looked at different organizing principles and ways of presenting the information. In the last analysis, I decided to maintain the original organization of the lessons: objectives, pre–reading, information, reading, and review. This, I concluded, was the best way for ESL students to receive, absorb, practice, and process new information. Because this organization is so important to the text, the co–authors of the original books, Deborah Short and Margaret Seufert, remain listed as co–authors of this book.

Those teachers familiar with the previous texts will find this new text very different. Many of the lessons have been deleted, new lessons have been created, and the exercises have been brought up–to–date. However, the basic facts about U.S. government, history, and civics remain the same.

I am grateful to the Center for Applied Linguistics, in Washington, D.C., for giving Delta Publishing Company permission to update and republish this text. I would also like to thank Lynda Franco and Jeannie Patchin for reviewing draft versions of this new book, and all the individuals who contributed to the original texts.

Allene Guss Grognet

LESSON 1

THE NEW WORLD

OBJECTIVE

- Identify major reasons why Europeans settled in North America

PRE–READING

Oral

Look at the map below. It shows the "Old World" and the "New World."

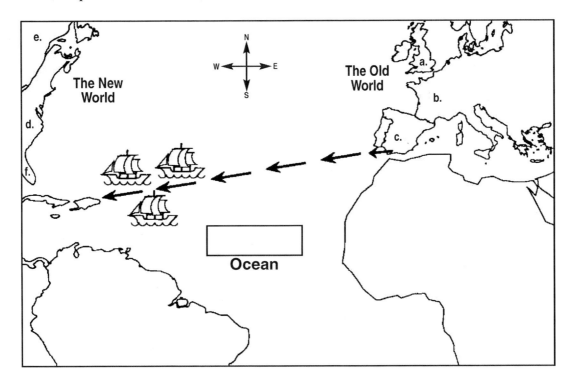

Work with a partner. Look at the map. Can you answer these questions?

1. What continents are part of the "Old World"?

2. What continents are part of the "New World"?

3. Can you name the ocean on the map? Write the name in the box.

4. Can you name any of the places? (a–e are now countries; f is now a state in the U.S.)

a.) _____   b.) _____   c.) _____

d.) _____   e.) _____   f.) _____

5. Who was one of the first men to go to America?

Map Skills

You will see many maps in this workbook. These words are for directions on a map:

North (N)   **East (E)**   **South (S)**   **West (W)**

You can also see:

Northeast (NE)   **Northwest (NW)**   **Southeast (SE)**   **Southwest (SW)**

Directions tell you the way to go. This is a symbol for directions:

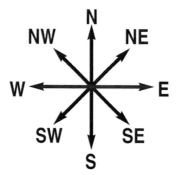

Read the questions below. Circle the letter of the best answer.

1. Look at the map again. Put a circle around c. This country is Spain. Put a circle around d. This country is the U.S. You are in Spain. Which way do you go to the U.S.?

   a) N   b) E   c) S   (d) W)

   (The correct answer is **d**. W = West.)

2. Put a circle around a. This country is England. You are in England. Which way do you go to Spain?

    a) N   b) E   c) S   d) W

3. Put a circle around e. This country is Canada. You are in the U.S. Which way do you go to Canada?

    a) N   b) E   c) S   d) W

4. Find the three boats in the Atlantic Ocean. Circle them. These are the boats (or ships) of Christopher Columbus. What direction are they going?

    a) NE   b) NW   c) SE   d) SW

Vocabulary

Read the following vocabulary words carefully. You will use them in this lesson and in other lessons.

Explorers travel to find new places. Many years ago explorers traveled by foot, by horse, and by boat.

A **discovery** is a new thing you find. For example, an explorer may find a new island. This island is a discovery.

Native Americans were the first people to live in North and South America. Sometimes we call them **Indians**.

(to) **settle**—to build a home and live in a new place. Many English people went to the New World and settled in North America.

(to) **trade**—to buy and sell things with another person or country. Early settlers traded food and clothing with England.

(to) **sail**—to go by boat with power from the wind. Columbus sailed across the Atlantic Ocean.

coast—the part of land near the ocean or sea. Settlers built the first towns in America near the coast.

INFORMATION: The Discovery of America

THE DISCOVERY OF AMERICA		
Explorer	**Major Area Explored**	**Why They Went**
Columbus	islands in the Caribbean	to find a new way to China
Spanish Explorers	Florida, Mexico, South America	to find gold and silver
French Explorers	Canada, northern part of the U.S.	1. to trade 2. to settle
English Explorers	east coast of North America	1. to trade 2. to have freedom of religion and to settle

Using the Information

A. The chart above gives you information about the first explorers of America. You will use many charts in this book. It is important to learn the best way to read a chart.

1. At the top of every chart, you will find a title. What is the title of this chart?

   _____

2. This chart has three columns. You read down a column. Each column has a heading. The heading tells you about the information in the column. The first column is about explorers. It lists the names of explorers or groups of explorers. How many names of explorers or groups do you see? _____

3. The second column tells you about the areas explored. Christopher Columbus explored some islands in the Caribbean.

   The Spanish explored Florida, Mexico, and _____.

   Where did the French explore? _____

4. What does the third column tell us? _____

5. Look at the whole chart. Read <u>across</u> on the same line. Why did Columbus sail to the Caribbean? _____

6. Who wanted to have freedom of religion? _____

B. The chart tells us some reasons for exploring and settling in new places. Work with a partner. Think about your reason for coming to America. Can you think of two or three other reasons? Write them below. Share your ideas with the class.

Reasons to Go to New Places

1) _____

2) _____

3) _____

READING: Exploring the New World

Columbus tried to sail from Spain to China in 1492. Spain is in Europe. China is in Asia. Columbus sailed across the Atlantic Ocean. He discovered some islands in the Caribbean. He was surprised. He did not know about North and South America.

After Columbus, many other explorers came to America. Spanish explorers settled in Florida and Mexico. Some went to South America. French explorers sailed north. They discovered Canada. English explorers sailed along the east coast of North America.

People came to the "New World" for many reasons. Four important reasons were:

1. trade
2. religious freedom
3. political freedom
4. finding gold and silver

In October, we celebrate **Columbus Day**. It is a national holiday.

Using the Reading

C. Read the following sentences. Some sentences are true and some sentences are false. Look at the information in the Reading. Put a **T** next to the true sentences. Put an **F** next to the false sentences.

1. ___T___ Columbus tried to go to China.

2. _____ Columbus explored Canada.

3. _____ Spanish explorers went to Mexico.

4. _____ English explorers settled on the West Coast of North America.

5. _____ Some people came to America to have religious freedom.

REVIEW

You will be asked questions at your USCIS interview. We will present the questions, and give you the answers. All the answers are in **bold face** in the lesson.

Question	**Answer**
1. Name <u>one</u> national U.S. holiday.	• Columbus Day

LESSON 2

TWO PERMANENT COLONIES

OBJECTIVES

- Identify the first two permanent colonies in America
- Identify the first national holiday, Thanksgiving

PRE–READING

Oral

Look at this map again.

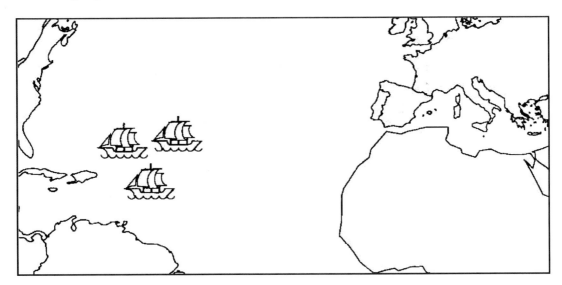

Your teacher will read the following paragraphs two times. Listen the first time. The second time, fill in the missing words. Use the map to help you.

English explorers left England. They sailed to the 1) _____. They

sailed across the 2) _____ Ocean. They settled on the 3) _____

coast of North America. French explorers left 4) _____. They went to the

"New World." They settled 5) _____ of the English settlers.

Vocabulary

Use these new words to complete the crossword puzzle below. You can use a dictionary to help you.

permanent   trader   Thanksgiving

Pilgrims   tobacco   colonies

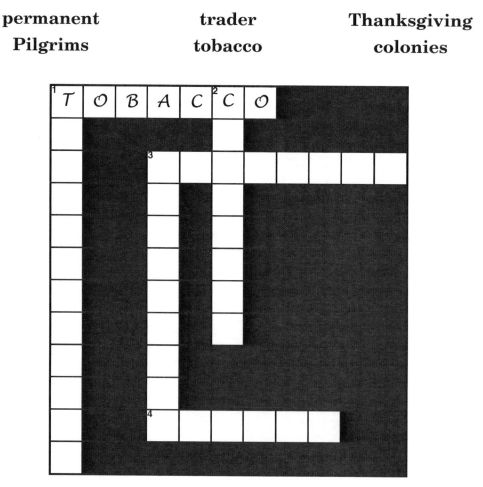

ACROSS

1 A common plant in the southeast U.S.; people use it in cigarettes

3 A religious group from England; they settled in Massachusetts

4 This person buys and sells things

DOWN

1 Americans celebrate this holiday in November; they have a very big dinner

2 A new place with settlers and a distant country controls the area, like a territory

3 Does not change; stays the same for a long time

INFORMATION: The First Two Colonies

This map shows the first two permanent English colonies in North America.

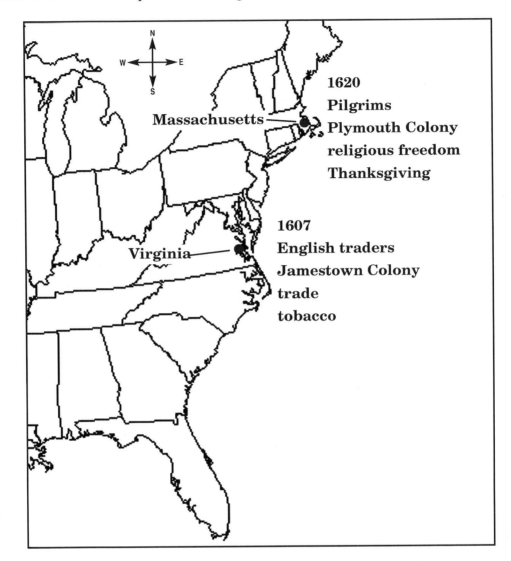

Using the Information

A. Work with a partner. Use the information above to complete the chart. Think of a title for the chart.

1.) Title: _____

Who	When	Name of Settlement	Reason for Coming
English traders 4.) _____	2.) _____ 1620	Jamestown Colony 5.) _____	3.) _____ religious freedom

B. Read sentences 1–3 to your partner. They are all false. Your partner tells you the true sentence. Use the map and chart to help you.

Here is an example:

YOU READ: Pilgrims settled in 1607. (*False*)
YOUR PARTNER SAYS: Pilgrims settled in 1620. (*True*)

1. Jamestown is north of Plymouth.

2. The Plymouth Colony is in Virginia.

3. The Pilgrims came to trade.

Now switch roles. Your partner reads sentences 4–6. You correct them. Use the map and chart.

4. The second colony was the Jamestown Colony.

5. The English traders came to America to have religious freedom.

6. Plymouth is on the West Coast of North America.

READING: Jamestown and Plymouth Colonies

English traders settled at Jamestown in Virginia in 1607. It was on the east coast of North America. These men wanted to trade with England. Their life at the Jamestown Colony was hard. At first, they did not have enough food. Many people died. They planted many things. Tobacco was the best plant. They traded it with England. They made money.

The Pilgrims left England in 1620. They wanted **religious freedom**. They sailed to America on a ship named the Mayflower. They settled at Plymouth Colony in Massachusetts. Their life was hard, too. Their winters were very cold. They did not have enough food. Many people died.

The Pilgrims did two important things:

1. They wrote the Mayflower Compact (an official paper). It said:
   a) the people decide the government rules, and
   b) the people follow the majority (51%) decision.

2. They celebrated the first **Thanksgiving**. They had a big dinner with the **Native Americans**. They wanted to thank the Native Americans for helping them. They were happy to be alive. **Thanksgiving** is the first American holiday.

Using the Reading

C. Write answers to the questions below.

1. Where was the first permanent English colony?

   _____

2. Was it easy to live at Jamestown and Plymouth?

   _____

3. What important plant did the settlers grow at Jamestown?

   _____

4. The Pilgrims wrote a paper to let the people decide about the government. What was the name of the official paper?

   _____

5. What holiday did the Pilgrims celebrate with Native Americans?

   _____

REVIEW

Question	**Answer**
1. What is <u>one</u> reason the colonists came to America?	• for religious freedom • for liberty • for opportunity
2. Who lived in America before the Europeans arrived?	• Native Americans (American Indians)
3. Name <u>one</u> national holiday. (You will be asked to name <u>two</u> holidays. Others are spread throughout book.)	• Thanksgiving

THE THIRTEEN COLONIES

OBJECTIVES

- Identify the 13 colonies
- Identify the early forms of government in the 13 colonies

PRE-READING

Oral

Look at this map. It is similar to the map in Lesson 2. That map had two colonies. This map has all 13 colonies on it. Work with a partner. Try to fill in the names of all these colonies. They are states in the U.S. now. You can use a map of the U.S. to help you. Compare your answers with the class.

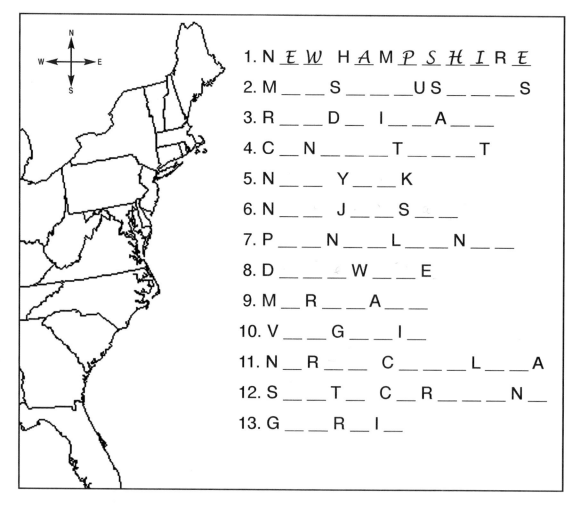

1. N _E_ _W_ H A _M_ P _S_ _H_ I R _E_
2. M _ _ S _ _ _ U S _ _ _ S
3. R _ _ D _ I _ _ A _ _
4. C _ N _ _ _ T _ _ _ T
5. N _ _ _ Y _ _ K
6. N _ _ _ J _ _ S _ _
7. P _ _ N _ _ L _ _ N _ _
8. D _ _ _ _ W _ _ E
9. M _ R _ _ A _ _ _
10. V _ _ G _ _ I _
11. N _ R _ _ _ C _ _ _ _ L _ _ A
12. S _ _ T _ C _ R _ _ _ N _
13. G _ _ R _ I _

Vocabulary

Read the following words and definitions.

representative assembly—a type of democracy. Settlers of a colony chose people to represent them at special meetings (assemblies). These people made some laws for the colony.

voters—male owners of property in the colonies could vote. Some colonies said a voter must be a certain religion.

(to) veto—to say "no"

King's Governor—the representative for the King of England in 11 of the colonies. The King's Governors could veto laws from the assemblies.

Puritans—another group of settlers in Massachusetts. They wanted religious freedom.

Quakers—a group of settlers in Pennsylvania and parts of Delaware and New Jersey. They wanted religious freedom.

separation of church and state—the church and government are separate. The government does not decide the rules of the church. The church does not decide the rules of the government.

Find the words on the left in the puzzle. Circle them.

	S	G	O	V	E	R	N	O	R	E	Q	P
Assembly	V	E	S	O	V	R	P	O	A	W	I	A
Voters	O	F	H	T	S	I	U	Y	N	Q	P	S
Quakers	R	C	V	E	T	O	R	E	U	U	B	S
Governor	T	G	I	R	A	M	I	T	E	A	N	E
Veto	G	O	V	S	L	Y	T	E	K	K	O	M
Puritans	C	I	C	O	M	P	A	C	T	E	Y	B
Compact	Q	U	A	K	L	U	N	S	E	R	V	L
	S	M	A	H	O	R	S	C	O	S	G	Y

INFORMATION: The Thirteen Colonies

THE NORTHERN COLONIES

New Hampshire

Settlers came from Massachusetts Colony.

They came for religious, political, and economic reasons.

Massachusetts

Pilgrims and Puritans settled there.

Pilgrims wrote the Mayflower Compact.

They came for religious freedom.

Rhode Island and Connecticut

Settlers came from the Massachusetts Colony.

They wanted religious freedom.

They believed in the separation of church and state.

THE MID–ATLANTIC COLONIES

New York

Dutch settlers came first.

English settlers took control later.

Many settlers wanted to trade.

New Jersey

Dutch and Swedish settlers came first.

They wanted to trade.

English settlers came later, especially Quakers.

They wanted religious freedom.

Pennsylvania

Quakers settled there for religious freedom.

They believed in the separation of church and state.

Delaware

This was part of Pennsylvania at first.

The settlers asked to have a separate government.

THE SOUTHERN COLONIES

Maryland
Catholic settlers came there for religious freedom.
A few people owned most of the land.
They rented and sold that land to make money.

Virginia
English traders settled there.
Jamestown was the first permanent colony.
Tobacco was an important plant to trade with Europe.

North and South Carolina
This was one colony at first.
A few people owned most of the land.
They rented and sold that land to make money.
Some French people came for religious freedom.

Georgia
Some poor people and people from English prisons settled here.

Using the Information

A. Fill in the blanks in the paragraph below. Look at the Information to find the missing words.

There were 1) ___thirteen (13)___ English colonies in North America. Four colonies

were in the north. They were New Hampshire, 2) _____, Rhode Island,

and Connecticut. Settlers in the northern colonies wanted religious 3) _____.

Dutch settlers lived in 4) _____ and New Jersey. Quakers settled in

Pennsylvania. The Quakers believed in the separation of 5) _____ and

state. Some settlers came to 6) _____ and North and South Carolina for

religious freedom. Settlers in Virginia wanted to sell 7) _____ to Europe.

READING: Democracy in the Colonies

There were two types of democracy in the colonies. Some colonies, like Virginia, had representative assemblies. The settlers did not vote directly. The settlers chose people (representatives) to go to the assembly meetings. These people represented the settlers. They voted about laws for their colony.

Other colonies, like Massachusetts, had direct democracies. Voters went to town meetings. They all voted about the laws for the town.

The colonists had two problems:

1. The King of England sent governors to 11 colonies. The governor could veto some laws from the assemblies and town meetings. The King could make other laws, too.

2. Some settlers could not vote. Voters needed to own property. Sometimes they had to be a certain religion to vote.

Using the Reading

B. Unscramble the following sentences. Look at the Reading to help you. The first word for each sentence is circled. The first sentence is done for you.

1. had / assembly / (Virginia) / representative / a

   Virginia had a representative assembly.

2. voted / (Representatives) / about laws / colonies / the / for

   _____

3. meetings / direct democracies / examples (Town) / are / of

   _____

4. (The)/ some laws / colonies / King of England / made / for / the

_____

C. Imagine your class is in a town in the Massachusetts Colony. Think about some problems in your town.

EXAMPLE: Some neighbors let their dogs run free. The dogs are running all over yards and killing plants.

Think of three more problems:

1. _____

2. _____

3. _____

Hold a town meeting. Try to solve one of the problems. Discuss possible solutions. Have a class vote.

REVIEW

Question	**Answer**
1. There were 13 original states? Name <u>three</u>.	• Massachusetts • Connecticut • Rhode Island • New Hampshire • New York • New Jersey • Pennsylvania • Maryland • Delaware • Virginia • Georgia • North Carolina • South Carolina

LESSON 4

THE COLONIES AND ENGLAND

OBJECTIVE

- Explain problems between the colonies and England

PRE–READING

Map Skills

Look at the map below. It shows French and English settlers in the New World.

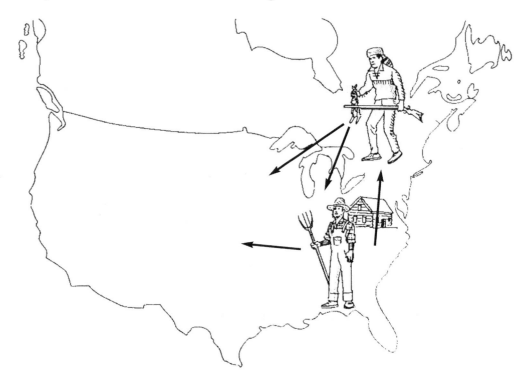

Which of the following do you think are true? Check (✔) them.

_____ 1. The English settlers lived in towns and on farms.

_____ 2. The French settlers wanted to move north.

_____ 3. The English settlers were hunters.

_____ 4. The English settlers wanted to move north and west.

_____ 5. The English and French made money different ways.

_____ 6. Most of the settlers lived along the coast.

_____ 7. The English and French did not try to move near each other.

Oral

Form a small group. Share your answers above. Do you all agree? Explain your answers.

The French want to move south. The English want to move north. What problems can happen?

Vocabulary

Match the words on the left with the definitions on the right. Put the correct letter on the line. You can use a dictionary for help.

___C___ 1. **fur**   a) made in a factory by machine

_____ 2. **trapper**   b) a group of people march and carry signs about something they do not like

_____ 3. **tax**   c) the hair on some animals; used to make a coat

_____ 4. (to) **boycott**   d) to stop buying something as a protest

_____ 5. **demonstration**   e) the legislature in England

_____ 6. **Parliament**   f) you pay this extra money to the government when you buy something

_____ 7. **manufactured**   g) things you have, or buy, or sell

_____ 8. **goods**   h) this person catches wild animals

Here are some other terms to learn:

Stamp Act—A law by Parliament for American colonists. The colonists had to buy stamps for all paper documents and newspapers.

Boarding and Quartering—the colonists had to house soldiers at any time.

Boston Tea Party—The Parliament also put a tax on tea. One night the colonists went on the English boats in the harbor at Boston, Massachusetts. They threw all the tea from the boats into the water. This was called the Boston Tea Party.

Information: A Timeline of Events in Colonial America

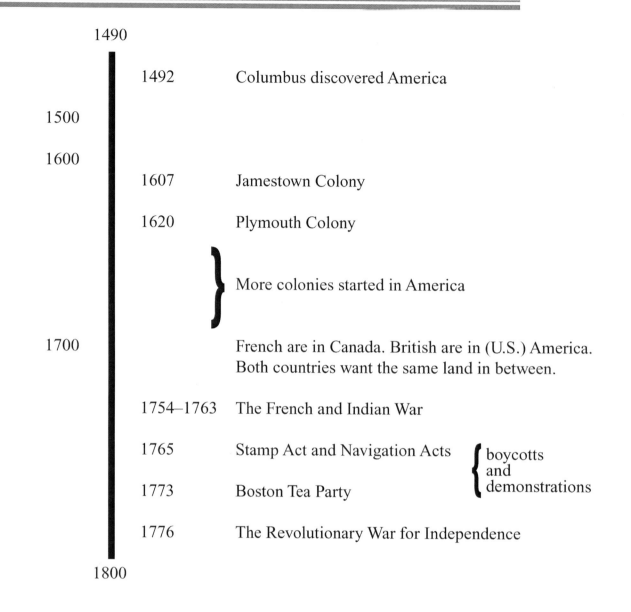

Using the Information

A. Timelines are useful for studying history. They show you the order of events. When you look at a timeline, you can see what happened first, second, etc.

1. Look at the above timeline. The dates on the left show the time period. This

timeline shows some important events from 1490 to _____.

2. The dates on the right show the year of the event. We can see Columbus came to

the Americas between 1490 and 1500. What was the exact year? _____.

Look at the timeline and try to answer these questions.

3. Which colony started first, Jamestown or Plymouth?_____

4. Did colonies start in Amcrica between 1500 and 1600 or between 1600 and 1700?

_____

5. Which happened first, the Boston Tea Party or the Navigation Acts?

_____

B. Find a partner. Make one timeline for both of you. Here are some ideas for dates:
- the year you were born
- the year you started school
- the year you got your first job
- the year you came to America
- the year you started this class

READING: Life in the Colonies Before the War for Independence

Many French were trappers and fur traders in the north (Canada). Many American colonists lived on farms and in towns in the south (U.S.). They were farmers, store owners, etc. The French and the English wanted the same land between the U.S. colonies and Canada. They fought the French and Indian War. The French and Indians were on one side. The English and the American colonists were on the other side. The English won the war. The French lost most of their colonies. Then England controlled Canada.

The war was expensive. The English wanted the colonists to help pay the costs. The English started new taxes. One tax law was the Stamp Act. Other laws dealt with **housing (quartering) soldiers**. The colonists were angry. They did not want to buy stamps for all documents. It was **taxation without representation**. They could not say "no" to the laws. They could not vote on the laws. They had no representative in Parliament.

The colonists took action. They boycotted English goods. They had demonstrations. They wrote letters to the newspapers. In 1773, the English also put a tax on tea. The colonists went on the tea ships in Boston Harbor and threw all the tea into the water. This was the "Boston Tea Party."

Using the Reading

C. Read the first sentence in the following questions. Look at the two choices. Which choice means the same as the first sentence? Circle the letter of the better answer.

EXAMPLE: Many French were fur traders in the north.
a) Many English were farmers in the south.
b) Many French worked as fur traders in the north.
(The correct answer is b.)

1. The French and the Indians were on one side.

   a) The French and the Indians fought together against the English.

   b) The French fought the Indians.

2. They had no representatives in Parliament.

   a) The colonists did not have a representative in the English legislature.

   b) The colonists voted for new tax laws.

3. The colonists boycotted English goods.

   a) The colonists did not buy things from England.

   b) The colonists paid taxes on English tea.

REVIEW

Question	Answer
1. Why did the colonists fight the British?	• Because of high taxes • Because of taxation without representation • Because British soldiers stayed in their houses • Because they didn't have self–government

LESSON 5

THE DECLARATION OF INDEPENDENCE

OBJECTIVE

- Identify the major principles of the Declaration of Independence

PRE-READING

Written

Sometimes it is important to read through information quickly. Scanning is an important reading skill. Scanning = reading quickly to find information. The following paragraph is the first part of the Declaration of Independence. Read it quickly (scan) and find the words below. Circle them in the paragraph.

truths   **equal**   **rights**   **liberty**   **powers**

"We hold these truths to be self–evident, that all men are created equal, that they are endowed by their Creator with certain inalienable rights, that among these are life, liberty and the pursuit of happiness. That to secure these rights, governments are instituted among men, deriving their just powers from the consent of the governed."

Oral

Discuss these questions with the class:

- Is your native country independent?

- If yes, when did your country become independent?

- If yes, did people in your country write a document like the Declaration of Independence?

- Why is it a good idea to write a declaration of independence?

- Whom do you think the colonists wrote the Declaration of Independence for?

Vocabulary

Use a dictionary. Write a definition for these words. The first one is done for you.

declaration— *a positive, explicit, or formal statement; proclamation;*

a document embodying or displaying an announcement or

proclamation—such as the Declaration of Independence.

(to) exist— _____

_____

_____

complaints— _____

_____

_____

united— _____

_____

_____

militia— _____

_____

_____

INFORMATION: The Declaration of Independence (1776)

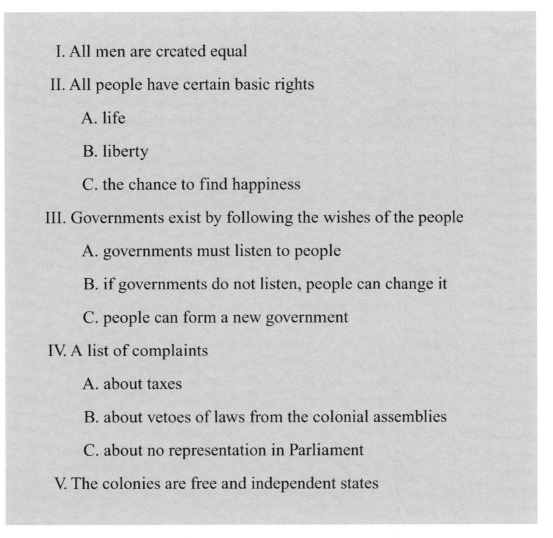

I. All men are created equal

II. All people have certain basic rights

    A. life

    B. liberty

    C. the chance to find happiness

III. Governments exist by following the wishes of the people

    A. governments must listen to people

    B. if governments do not listen, people can change it

    C. people can form a new government

IV. A list of complaints

    A. about taxes

    B. about vetoes of laws from the colonial assemblies

    C. about no representation in Parliament

V. The colonies are free and independent states

Using the Information

A. The Declaration of Independence is an important document. The Information above shows the important ideas of the document in an outline.

Outlines are useful for studying. You can see the main points with an outline. You can also get examples or additional information for the main points. The outline form is easy to read. Usually outlines have Roman numerals for the main points. These are like numbers: I = 1 (one), II = 2 (two), III = 3 (three), IV = 4 (four), etc.

Look at the Information. There are five main points in the Declaration of Independence. These points are:

I. All men are created equal

II. All people have certain b __ s __ __   r i __ __ t __

III. G __ v __ __ n m __ __ __ s exist by following the wishes of the p __ __ __ l __

IV. A list of c __ __ p __ __ __ n __ __

V. The colonies are __ __ __ __ and __ __ __ __ __ __ __ __ __ __ __ states

The Declaration of Independence lists three examples of basic rights. Look at part II. What are the three examples?

a) _____

b) _____

c) _____

Look at part III. This part gives more information about one of the main points.

d) What must governments do? _____

e) Can the people form a new government? _____

f) Does part IV give examples of complaints? _____

g) If yes, how many examples are there? _____

h) Name one complaint. _____

B. The Declaration of Independence says, "All men are created equal." Do you think this is true? In the U.S., people did not always treat everyone equally. For example, for many years women did not have the right to vote.

Work with a partner. Think of other examples where people do not have equal rights. Use examples from the U.S. and your country. List them in the following chart.

COUNTRY	SITUATION
U.S.	Women did not have the right to vote in 1776.

READING: Writing the Declaration of Independence

Representatives from 12 of the 13 colonies came to a very important meeting in Philadelphia, Pennsylvania. They asked **Thomas Jefferson** to write the Declaration of Independence. It said that all men are created equal. It also said that they have rights to life, liberty and the pursuit of happiness and must follow the wishes of the people. Representatives of all 13 Colonies signed it on **July 4, 1776**. It made the colonies **free from England**. The 4th of July is a holiday now. We call it **Independence Day**.

Using the Reading

C. Circle the letter of the correct answer.

1. Who wrote the Declaration of Independence?

   a) George Washington   b) Thomas Jefferson   c) Parliament

2. Which one is a basic right in the Declaration of Independence?

   a) liberty   b) a new government   c) taxes

3. How many colonies had representatives to sign the Declaration of Independence?

   a) 12   b) 13   c) 17

REVIEW

Question	**Answer**
1. What did the Declaration of Independence do?	• Said that the U.S. is free from England
2. When was the Declaration of Independence adopted?	• July 4,1776
3. When do we celebrate Independence Day?	• July 4th
4. Who wrote the Declaration of Independence?	• Thomas Jefferson

THE FIRST PRESIDENT

OBJECTIVES

- Identify the first president of the U.S.
- Identify the Presidents' Day holiday

PRE-READING

Oral

Look at the picture below. He is a famous American.

Work with a partner. Who is the person in the picture? What do you know about him? List three things.

1. _____

2. _____

3. _____

Share your list with the class.

We call the leader of the United States the **president**. What do you call the leader in your country?

Vocabulary

Read the following words and definitions.

Cabinet—a group of advisors to the president

U.S. foreign policy—the way the U.S. government plans to act with other countries of the world

Secretary of the Treasury—one of the Cabinet members, head of the Treasury Department. The Treasury Department collects taxes and controls the money.

Secretary of State—one of the Cabinet members, head of the State Department. The State Department helps plan U.S. foreign policy.

Secretary of War—one of the Cabinet members, responsible for the army and navy. (Now this person is called the Secretary of Defense.)

Attorney General—one of the Cabinet members, head of the Justice Department. The Justice Department makes sure people in the U.S. follow the laws.

Farewell Address—a public talk by the president at the end of his term

precedent—an example or rule to follow in a similar future situation

isolation—a policy of being alone or separated from others

unanimous—everyone agrees to something; no opposition

INFORMATION: George Washington (1732—1799)

Commander–in–Chief	Father of Our Country
• Fought in French & Indian War • Head of American militia in Revolutionary War • Head of the army and navy as president	• Hero in Revolutionary War • Leader of the Constitutional Convention • Signer of the Constitution • National Holiday: Presidents' Day

President (1789–1797)

- Unanimous election—first president of the U.S.
- Set up Cabinet: Departments of State, War, the Treasury and Attorney General
- Two terms in office
- Wanted a loose interpretation of the Constitution
- Farewell address—wanted American isolation from European problems

Using the Information

A. Match the second part of the sentence (on the right) with the first part of the sentence (on the left). Put the correct letter on the line.

__*d*__ 1. George Washington fought

a) he was 65 years old.

_____ 2. Washington set up a Cabinet

b) in two wars.

_____ 3. Washington was the leader of the American army

c) because the election was unanimous.

_____ 4. In Washington's Farewell Address

d) during and after the Revolutionary War.

_____ 5. When Washington left after two terms as President

e) he discussed U.S. foreign policy.

_____ 6. We know the people wanted Washington to be the first President

f) with four departments.

B. Form a small group. Think about the leader of your country. What do you think are some strong points for a good leader?

These were some strong points for George Washington:
- able to make compromises
- brave man
- good military chief
- had new and good ideas about the presidency (like the Cabinet)

Make a list of other strong points for a leader:

1. _____

2. _____

3. _____

READING: The Life of George Washington

George Washington was born in 1732. He grew up in the Virginia Colony. During the French and Indian War, he fought with the British. He was a good soldier.

Washington wanted the American colonies to be independent. He agreed to become the chief of the militia in the Revolutionary War against the British. He taught the men in the militia many things about fighting. He trained the men well. The colonies won the war.

In 1789 **Washington became the first president of the U.S.** All the representatives voted for him. No one voted against him. His election was unanimous. He also became the first **commander–in–chief of the army and navy**.

He did not want to be like a king. He asked people to help him. They were his advisors, or Cabinet members. Now every president has a Cabinet. Washington's Cabinet had four members: Secretary of State, Secretary of War, Secretary of the Treasury, and Attorney General. The number of secretaries can change. Today (2009), the Cabinet has 15 members.

Washington was elected for a second term. But, he decided to leave the office of president after the second time. Washington also gave an important Farewell Address. In his talk, he gave ideas for U.S. foreign policy. He suggested American isolation. He did not want the U.S. to become part of European problems. He knew the U.S. had problems itself, and Americans had to help make their own country better first.

George Washington lived at Mount Vernon in Virginia after the presidency. He died in 1799. Washington was a great man. Americans call him the **"Father of Our Country."** We remember him on **Presidents' Day**. It is a national holiday in February.

Using the Reading

C. Complete the following outline about George Washington's life. Use the information in the Reading to help you.

George Washington was born in the year _____. He lived in

_____. He was elected the _____

president. He was also named _____

of the army and navy. He spent _____ in office. We call

him _____ and

celebrate _____ to honor him.

REVIEW

Question	**Answer**
1. Who was the first president of the United States?	• George Washington
2. Name <u>one</u> U.S. national holiday.	• Presidents' Day
3. Who is the "Father of Our Country?"	• George Washington

LESSON 7

THE CONSTITUTIONAL CONVENTION

OBJECTIVES

- Explain the reasons for writing the Constitution
- Explain the compromises in the Constitution

PRE–READING

Written

Read the questions below. Scan the following paragraph quickly and answer these questions. Circle **Y** (yes) or **N** (no).

1. Did the states want to change the articles?	Y	N
2. Did the representatives to the convention meet in Washington, D.C.?	Y	N
3. Did all 13 states send representatives to the convention?	Y	N
4. Did the central government have problems with the Articles of Convention?	Y	N

The states decided to change the Articles of Confederation. The central government had too many problems. The states acted like individual countries. Representatives from 12 states met in Philadelphia for a convention. They had many discussions about new ideas for the government. They wrote new rules. They called these rules the "Constitution."

Vocabulary

Read the following words and definitions.

Constitution—the official document of the rules for the U.S. government

convention—a large meeting of people, usually for several days or a week

compromise—a difficult agreement; different groups use only parts of their ideas for the final decision

debate—a discussion between two people or groups with different ideas or opinions; both people or groups tell their ideas

tariff—a tax on foreign goods sold in the U.S.

loose interpretation of the Constitution—a plan for understanding and following the Constitution. The Constitution does not list all the rules for the government. A loose interpretation lets the central government have more powers (when necessary) than the ones listed in the Constitution.

strict interpretation of the Constitution—a plan for understanding and following the Constitution. The Constitution does not list all the rules for the government. A strict interpretation tells the central government it can use only the powers listed in the Constitution. Other powers are for the state governments and the people.

INFORMATION: **Constitutional Convention Compromises**

The representatives at the Constitutional Convention wanted to change the Articles of Confederation. **They decided to write the Constitution,** but it was not easy. Different states had different ideas about a new government. The representatives had many debates. They told their opinions. They tried to think about good things for the country.

These are some ideas and compromises made at the convention:

Debate: An Executive

Yes
Some representatives wanted one person or a group of people to be the head of the government.

No
Some representatives did not want any head of government. They did not want someone to become president for life, like a king.

Compromise: A President
One person would be president.
The term in office would be four years.
Americans would have a new election every four years.

Debate: Representation in Congress

Virginia Plan (large states)
state population decides the number of representatives

New Jersey Plan (small states)
equal number of representatives from each state

Compromise: Have a congress with two houses

House of Representatives
state population determines the number of representatives
term: 2 years

Senate
two representatives for each state
term: 6 years

Debate: Tariffs

South
Farmers did not want taxes put on goods they sold to foreign countries.

North
Factory workers wanted the central government to control trade and protect U.S. goods.

Compromise: Trade Rules
The central government controls foreign trade,
can put tariffs on foreign goods,
but cannot put taxes on U.S. goods
sold to foreign countries

Using the Information

A   Unscramble the following sentences about the convention. The first word of every sentence has a capital letter.

1. representatives / debates / The / many / had

_____

2. about representation / important / compromise / The / very / was

_____

3. senators / sends / state / to / Every / Congress / two

_____

4. wanted / North / foreign / taxes / The / goods / on

_____

B. Role play a debate at the convention. Form two groups and divide into two sides. Choose a present situation like:

   • the speed limit on highways, or
   • the age for buying alcohol.

Try to think of some other situations:

1. _____

2. _____

Plan a debate. Each side discusses its opinion about the situation. Give your reasons.

READING: Debate About the Constitution

It was not easy to write the Constitution. Different representatives had many ideas. They had discussions and debates about the situations in the U.S. Sometimes the South wanted one thing and the North wanted another thing. The men wrote the Constitution slowly and carefully. They wanted it to last for a long time.

The Constitution was not accepted by all Americans immediately. After the representatives at the convention agreed to it, each state government had to vote on it. Now all the people could discuss the ideas in the Constitution. People wrote letters to the newspapers about their opinions.

Many people were interested in the Constitution. Two groups formed. They were the Federalists and the anti–Federalists. **The Federalists wanted the states to accept the Constitution**. They believed in a loose interpretation of the Constitution. **James Madison of Virginia, Alexander Hamilton of New York, and John Jay of New York** were some of the Federalists. The anti–Federalists wanted to make sure their rights and liberties were included in the Constitution. They wanted a strict interpretation.

The **oldest member** of the Constitutional Convention was **Benjamin Franklin**. He had been a **diplomat to France and England** and was famous for writing **Poor Richard's Almanac**. He added wisdom to the Convention.

The representatives signed the Constitution in **1787**. The debate in the 13 states lasted 3 years. Finally, all the state governments accepted the Constitution by 1790. The Constitution became the official rules of the U.S. government.

Using the Reading

C. All of the following sentences are false. Write the true sentences.

1. The representatives wrote the Constitution quickly.

_____

_____

2. The representatives did not have any disagreements about the Constitution.

_____

_____

3. When all the representatives signed the Constitution, it became the official rules for the U.S. government.

_____

_____

4. The Constitution is important because it tells about the U.S. war for independence.

_____

_____

REVIEW

Question	Answer
1. What happened at the Constitutional Convention?	• The Constitution was written
2. When was the Constitution written?	•1787
3. The Federalist Papers supported the passage of the U.S. Constitution. Name <u>one</u> of the writers.	• James Madison • Alexander Hamilton • John Jay
4. What is <u>one</u> thing Benjamin Franklin is famous for?	• U.S. diplomat • oldest member of the Constitutional Convention • writer

LESSON 8

THE CONSTITUTION—
THE SUPREME LAW OF THE LAND

OBJECTIVES

- Explain the concept of a constitution
- Identify the three main principles of the Constitution

PRE-READING

Oral

Look at the chart below. It lists important ideas in the U.S. Constitution.

<u>1787</u>

"We the People"

supreme law of the land

self-government

basic rights

Discuss the following questions with the class.

1. Does your country or the country your family came from have a constitution?

2. How old is your constitution?

3. How old is the U.S. Constitution?

4. What ideas are in a constitution?

Written

Read the following sentences. Do you think they are true (T) or false (F)? Circle **T** or **F**.

1. The Constitution is very important in the U.S.	T	F
2. The Constitution tells us about basic rights.	T	F
3. The President makes all the laws in the U.S.	T	F
4. We write a new constitution every 100 years.	T	F

Vocabulary

Use the following vocabulary words to finish the crossword puzzle. You can use a dictionary to help you.

representative	supreme	government	guarantee
branch	protects	property	trial

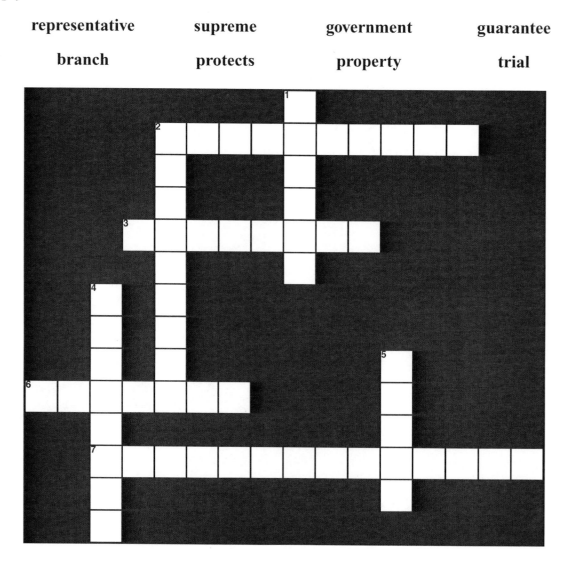

ACROSS

2 **Ruling a country by the people is self–**__ __ __ __ __ __ __ __ __ __

3 **Defends =** __ __ __ __ __ __ __ __

6 **The highest =** __ __ __ __ __ __ __ __

7 **Someone acting in your place =** __ __ __ __ __ __ __ __ __ __ __ __ __ __

DOWN

1 **Part of the U. S. government = a** __ __ __ __ __ __ **of the U.S. government**

2 **Promise =** __ __ __ __ __ __ __ __ __

4 **Possession, something you own =** __ __ __ __ __ __ __ __

5 **Legal action in court =** __ __ __ __ __

INFORMATION: Three Main Principles of the Constitution

1. Basic Rights	2. Government by the People	3. Separation of Powers
Freedom of speech Freedom of religion Right to have a trial Right to own property	People vote for their representatives People can ask for new laws or changes	Three branches of government with different powers **Checks and balances**

Using the Information

A. Complete the following paragraph. Use these words:

second	by	principles	check	three
religion	basic	balance	different	

There are three main 1) __*principles*__ of the U.S. Constitution. The first one

guarantees 2) _____ rights. It gives us freedom of speech and

3) _____. The 4) _____ principle tells about a

government 5) _____ the people. The third principle tells about the

6) _____ branches of the U.S. government. These branches have

7) _____ powers. They 8) _____ and

9) _____ each other.

B. Form small groups. Talk about rules for your class. Which rules are very important? Talk about your rights as students. Write the important rules and rights as a group constitution. Share your constitution with the class. Try to write a class constitution together.

READING: The Supreme Law

The U. S. Constitution is the **supreme law** of the country. Written **in 1787, it defines the government**. We cannot make any other laws against the Constitution. It tells us the important rules of our country. It tells us **that everyone must obey the law. No one is above the law**.

The Constitution protects the rights of all the people living in the U.S. Everyone must follow the Constitution or they can get into trouble. We have self–government in the federal, state, and local governments because we choose representatives. The representatives can make laws or change laws.

Using the Reading

C. Look again at the Reading and the chart on page 43, then at the true and false questions on page 41. Can you answer them correctly now? Circle **T** or **F**.

1. The Constitution is very important in the U.S.	T	F
2. The Constitution tells us about basic rights.	T	F
3. The President makes all the laws in the U.S.	T	F
4. We write a new constitution every 100 years.	T	F

Here are some more true / false questions.

5. We have self–government only at the federal level.	T	F
6. Some laws are more important than the Constitution.	T	F
7. Representatives can make changes in the laws.	T	F
8. The Constitution says that we can own property.	T	F

REVIEW

Question	**Answer**
1. What does the Constitution do?	• Defines the government • Sets up the government • Protects basic rights
2. What is the rule of law?	• Everyone must follow the law • No one is above the law • Leaders and government must obey the law
3. When was the Constitution written?	• 1787
4. What is the supreme law of the land?	• The Constitution
5. What stops one branch of government from becoming too powerful?	• Separation of powers • Checks and balances

LESSON 9

THE CONSTITUTION—
THE PREAMBLE

OBJECTIVES

- Describe the structure of the Constitution
- Identify the Preamble

PRE–READING

Oral

Discuss these questions with the class:

You want to know about a TV show tonight. How can you find out about it?

Suppose you want to go to a movie this weekend. There are two movies near your house. How can you find out about them?

You go to the library. You want a book to read. How can you learn about the story before you read it?

What is an introduction? Is it important? Why or why not?

Written

Read the following paragraph quickly to find the following words. Underline them.

welfare   **justice**   **defense**   **establish**

PREAMBLE

We the people of the United States, in order to form a more perfect Union, establish justice,

ensure domestic tranquility, provide for the common defense, promote the general welfare,

and secure the blessings of liberty to ourselves and our posterity, do ordain and establish

this Constitution for the United States of America.

Vocabulary

Match the words on the left with the meaning on the right. Put the correct letter on the line. You can use a dictionary to help you.

__C__ 1. (to) **establish**   a) peace, calm, quiet

_____ 2. (to) **ordain**   b) doing well in life

_____ 3. **justice**   c) to set up, to start

_____ 4. **domestic**   d) protection

_____ 5. **tranquility**   e) children, grandchildren, etc.

_____ 6. **posterity**   f) about the home or native land

_____ 7. **defense**   g) equal, fair action

_____ 8. **welfare**   h) good wishes

_____ 9. **blessings**   i) to order as a law

INFORMATION: Parts of the Constitution

> **Preamble = Introduction**
>
> **Articles 1–7 = Main points**
>
> **Amendments = Additions and changes**

PREAMBLE

You read the original Preamble in the beginning of the lesson. Here is another way to write the Preamble:

We are the people of the United States. We are writing this Constitution to have a better country. We want to set up a system of justice and to have peace in the country. We want to have an army to defend our country. We want to help people have a good life and to have liberty for ourselves and our children.

Using the Information

A. Check (✔) the sentences that tell about the Preamble.

_____ 1. It is the introduction of the Constitution.

_____ 2. It gives additions and changes to the Constitution.

_____ 3. It says the citizens want a better country.

_____ 4. It says the people want peace in the country.

_____ 5. It says the people do not want an army to protect the country.

_____ 6. It says the people want freedom for their children.

REVIEW

Question

1. The idea of self–government is in the first three words (introduction) of the Constitution. What are these words?

Answer

• We the people…

LESSON 10

THE CONSTITUTION— THE ARTICLES

OBJECTIVE

- Identify the content of different articles in the Constitution

PRE-READING

Oral

Look at these pictures of important buildings. They have special meanings for Americans. Each building represents a branch of the federal government. Can you identify the buildings?

Many people work in these buildings.

1. Do you know any duties they have?

2. Do you think one branch has more power than the other two branches?

3. Do you have any contact with the federal government?

Vocabulary

Read the following words and definitions.

Legislative part of the government—the Congress (the House of Representatives + the Senate for the federal government)

Executive part of the government—the president, vice president, and his helpers (or advisors) for the federal government

Judicial part of the government—the Supreme Court, other courts, and their judges

To **amend** the Constitution—to make some changes, to add some new things

To **ratify** the Constitution or an amendment—when three–fourths (¾) of the states vote "yes"

Treaty–when the United States says it will do something or will not do something, together with another country, the president can suggest a treaty. The Senate must approve, or say "okay" to the treaty.

Written

Read the vocabulary. Circle the word that does not belong.

> **Example:**   school   student   (car)   desk
> **Answer:** car (because school, student, and desk are words about education)

1. Congress	Senate	Legislative	Preamble
2. Changes	Treaties	Additions	Amendments
3. Representatives	White House	Vice President	Executive
4. Judicial	Judges	Ratify	Courts

INFORMATION: Articles of the Constitution

The writers of the Constitution used Roman numerals for numbers. I = 1, II = 2, III = 3, IV = 4, V = 5, VI = 6, VII = 7. The names are the same: I = "one," V = "five."

ARTICLE	WHO	WHAT IT DOES
I	Legislative	• makes laws and decides taxes • okays treaties
II	Executive	• gives ideas for laws and treaties • is Chief of Army and Navy (president)
III	Judicial	• decides if laws are okay (judges) • helps protect people's rights
IV	States	• says all states have a republican form of government • tells each state to respect the laws of another state
V		• tells how to amend the Constitution
VI		• says the Constitution is the supreme law
VII		• tells how to ratify the Constitution

Using the Information

A. Look at the chart and vocabulary. Fill in the blanks.

1. There are _____ articles in the Constitution.

2. Article I talks about the Congress or the House of _____ and

   the _____. They can _____ taxes and make new

   _____.

3. The president is the _____ of the army.

4. Information about the courts is in Article _____.

5. Article V says the government can change the Constitution.

   _____–fourths of the states must vote to pass an amendment.

B. Work with a partner. One person reads the five sentences. They are not true. The other person listens and makes them true.

1. The president okays treaties.

2. Article V tells us each state has a republican form of government.

3. The Senate decides if laws are okay.

4. Article IV tells about ratifying the Constitution.

5. The judicial part of the government decides taxes.

READING: The Articles of the Constitution

Article I. The Congress has many powers. **It makes federal laws.** It can decide taxes like the Social Security tax. It also makes laws about citizenship. Congress can start post offices, too. It makes laws about foreign trade. For example, if Honda, from Japan, wants to sell more cars in the U.S., the Congress decides yes or no. If the U.S. fights with another country, Congress can declare war.

Article II. The president has other powers. **He or she is the Commander–in–Chief of the military.** The president can choose people to be judges on the Supreme Court. He or she can choose people to be ambassadors. But, the Senate must say okay to these people. The president also gives information to the Congress. He or she tells Congress about problems in the U.S.

Article III. The Judicial branch has certain powers. **The courts can review some laws. They can explain the law. If the laws do not agree with the Constitution, the courts can tell Congress to change the laws.** The courts listen to problems about protecting the Constitutional rights of the people.

Article IV. States have a republican form of government. States can make some state laws. All states must respect the laws of other states. If Congress says okay, new states can become part of the U.S.

Article V. This article explains the way to **amend** (change) the Constitution. Three–fourths of the states must say okay to an **amendment.**

Article VI. This article says **the Constitution is the supreme law of the U.S.** Everyone must follow the Constitution.

Article VII. This article says three–fourths of the states must say okay to this Constitution. There were only 13 states in 1787.

Using the Reading

  C. These sentences are about Articles I (legislative), II (executive), III (judicial), and IV (states). Put the number I, II, III, or IV next to the sentence that describes that Article.

   _____ 1. Tells about citizenship laws.

   _____ 2. Tells about protecting our rights.

   _____ 3. Tells about choosing judges.

   _____ 4. Tells about setting up places to mail letters and buy stamps.

   _____ 5. Tells about setting up new states.

   _____ 6. Tells about business with foreign countries.

   _____ 7. Tells about the head of the army.

REVIEW

Question	Answer
1. What is an amendment?	• a change to the Constitution • an addition to the Constitution
2. Who is commander–in–chief of the military?	• the president
3. What is the supreme law of the land?	• the Constitution
4. Who makes federal laws?	• Congress • the Senate and the House of Representatives
5. What does the judicial branch do?	• reviews laws • explains laws • decides if laws go against the Constitution
6. Name <u>one</u> branch (or part) of the government.	• Congress (legislative) • Executive (President) • Judicial (courts)

THE CONSTITUTION—
THE BILL OF RIGHTS
(AMENDMENTS 1–10)

OBJECTIVES

- Identify the Bill of Rights (Amendments 1–10)
- Show the importance of the Bill of Rights to all the people living in the U.S.

PRE–READING

Oral

Form a small group. Discuss the following situations. Record a group answer and share it with the class.

1. Jose wants to put a sign on his car, "VOTE FOR PABLO VELASQUEZ." Can he do this?

2. Carmen is a member of the Baptist Church. Is that okay in the U.S.?

3. The police stop Jean–Pierre. They take him to the station. Can he talk to a lawyer?

4. The police put Jean–Pierre in jail. He does not know why. He stays there for three years before he goes to trial. Is this okay in the U.S.?

5. A group of people in Arizona do not like a new law about buying guns. Can they tell the president they do not like the law? Can they write their opinion in the newspaper?

Vocabulary

Use the following words to complete the crossword puzzle. The definitions are below. You can use a dictionary to help you.

unfair

accused

lawyer

fine

witnesses

interfere

search

punishment

bail

amendments

ACROSS

1 _ _ _ _ _ _ _ —to look for something

3 _ _ _ _ _ _ _ _ —when someone says you did something wrong

4 _ _ _ _ _ —money you pay the court so you do not have to stay in jail while you
wait for your day in court

7 _ _ _ _ _ _ _ _ _ _ _ —going to jail or paying a fine is an example of this

9 _ _ _ _ _ _ _ _ _ _ — people who speak in your favor or against you in court;
they tell the court what they saw or what they know

10 _ _ _ _ _ _ _ —a person who studies the laws and court systems; he/she can
help you in court or with other problems, like immigration

DOWN

2 _ _ _ _ _ _ _ _ _ _ _ —when something is added or changed (amended) in the
Constitution, it is added as these

5 _ _ _ _ _ _ _ _ _ —to get in the way; to make problems

6 _ _ _ _ —the money you must pay because you did something wrong

8 _ _ _ _ _ _ —not appropriate; too much or too little

INFORMATION: The Bill of Rights (Amendments 1–10)

The Bill of Rights are the **first 10 amendments** to the Constitution.

Amendment 1. Freedom of Religion, Speech, the Press, and Assembly

> **We can follow any religion**; we can say our thoughts; we can write articles in newspapers; we can meet in groups.

Amendment 2. The Right to Have Guns

> We can have guns for protection. State governments make laws about buying and keeping guns.

Amendment 3. Housing Soldiers

> We do not have to let soldiers stay in our homes in peace time. If there is a war, Congress can pass a law to let soldiers stay in our homes.

Amendment 4. Searches and Warrants

> Police need a court order (search warrant) to search our homes or to take our things.

Amendment 5. Rights of People Accused of a Crime, and Protection of Private Property

> If a judge says you are free at a trial, you do not go to a second trial for the same crime. You do not have to answer questions at your trial. The government must pay a fair price before taking private property from someone.

Amendment 6. Right to a Fair Trial and Witnesses

> If you are accused of a crime, you have the right to know why. You have the right to a speedy and public trial with a jury. You have the trial in the state where the crime happened. You can have a private lawyer or the court will give you a lawyer. The lawyers can question all the witnesses. You can have witnesses on your side.

Amendment 7. Right to a Jury Trial

> If the money in your case is over twenty dollars ($20.00), you can have a jury trial.

Amendment 8. Bails, Fines, and Punishments

> A judge cannot make you pay an unfair bail. A judge or jury cannot make you pay an unfair fine. A judge or jury or the police cannot give you unfair punishment.

Amendment 9. The People Keep Some Rights

> The Constitution lists many rights of the people, but it does not list all the rights. The people have other rights, too.

Amendment 10. The States or People Keep Some Powers

> The Constitution lists some powers for the federal government, but it cannot list all the powers. The other powers are for the states or for the people.

Using the Information

A. Read the following sentences about rights. Which amendment gives you each right? Put the number of the amendment next to the sentence about it.

1.) __4__ A policeman shows you a court order and he comes into your apartment.

2.) _____ A TV newswoman does not like a treaty the president made with China. On TV, she says the treaty is bad.

3.) _____ The people have some rights that are not written in the Constitution.

4.) _____ You must complete an application form and wait 7 days if you want to buy a gun in the state of Maryland.

5.) _____ A poor man does not have money for a lawyer. The court gives him a lawyer.

6.) _____ The police must tell you why they are taking you to the police station.

7.) _____ The court says you are wrong. You must go to jail for 5 years.

B. Work with a partner. Discuss these questions. Share your answers with the class.

1. Does your country have jury trials?

2. Does your country put people in jail without trials?

3. Do the people have freedom of speech in your country?

4. Can you name a country without religious freedom?

5. Do you think the Bill of Rights is important? Why or why not?

READING: Freedom

Freedom is the most important right we have in the U.S. In the 1600's, people came to find freedom. What is freedom?

Freedom means you can...

- follow any religion
- say and write your ideas
- choose your type of work
- have meetings when you want
- live where you want
- ask the government to make changes
- live in peace

The U.S. Constitution and the U.S. government protect the rights and freedom of **all the people** living in the U.S. No one can interfere with the rights of other people. No one can take away your rights if you follow the law. We should all follow the laws and protect everyone's rights.

Using the Reading

C. Form a small group. Read and discuss the following sentence. What do you think it means? Share your group's ideas with the class.

"My freedom ends where your freedom begins."

REVIEW

Question	Answer
1. What is an Amendment?	• a change or addition to the Constitution
2. What is the Bill of Rights?	• The first 10 Amendments
3. What do we call first 10 amendments to the Constitution?	• The Bill of Rights
4. What is <u>one</u> right or freedom from the First Amendment?	• religion • assembly • the press • speech • petition the government
5. What is freedom of religion?	• You can practice (or not practice) any religion
6. What are <u>two</u> rights of everyone living in the U.S.?	• freedom of speech • freedom of assembly • freedom of religion • freedom to bear arms

LESSON 12

THE CONSTITUTION—
THE OTHER AMENDMENTS
(11–27)

OBJECTIVES

- Identify purposes of Amendments 11–27
- Discuss the importance of the amendment process

PRE–READING

Oral

Look at the following pictures. What is happening? Does the Constitution discuss these situations?

Vocabulary

Use a dictionary. Find the meaning of these words.

slavery—_____

_____

(to) repeal—_____

_____

(to) **resign** (from a job)—_____

_____

restrictions _____

_____

Written

Read the questions below. Then look at the Information. Scan it to find the answers. Circle **Y** (yes) or **N** (no).

    Example: Look at Amendment 13. Can we have slavery in the U.S.?   Y   Ⓝ

    1. Look at Amendment 15. Can black people vote?   Y   N

    2. Do some of the amendments tell us who can vote?   Y   N

    3. Do some of the amendments discuss electing a President?   Y   N

    4. Do some of the amendments discuss taxes?   Y   N

INFORMATION: Amendments 11–27

Amendment 11. Citizens of one state or a foreign country cannot bring a case against another state in a federal court.

Amendment 12. We elect the president and vice president separately.

Amendment 13. There is no more slavery in the U.S.

Amendment 14. All people born or naturalized in the U.S. are citizens.

Amendment 15. Black people have the right to vote.

Amendment 16. Congress can make a law for an income tax.

Amendment 17. We elect senators directly with our votes.

Amendment 18. It is illegal to make or sell liquor in the U.S.

Amendment 19. Women have the right to vote.

Amendment 20. A new president takes office on January 20.

Amendment 21. This repeals the 18th Amendment. Now it is legal to make or sell liquor in the U.S.

Amendment 22. We can elect the same president for two terms. Each term is for 4 years.

Amendment 23. Citizens of Washington, D.C. (District of Columbia), can vote for president and vice president.

Amendment 24. We do not have to pay a voting tax.

Amendment 25. If the president dies or resigns, the vice president becomes president. If both the president and the vice president cannot serve, the Speaker of the House becomes president. This amendment also tells the order for other important government officials to become president if something happens to the vice president, etc.

Amendment 26. Citizens 18 years old or older can vote.

Amendment 27. Congress can raise its pay, but it must wait for the next election before the increase becomes effective.

Using the Information

A. Form a small group. Discuss the following pictures. What do the pictures tell us about the amendments?

B. Organize Amendments 11–27 into the following categories. List the numbers of the amendments:

VOTING / ELECTIONS

1.) _____

2.) _____

3.) _____

4.) _____

5.) _____

6.) _____

7.) _____

8.) _____

PRESIDENT ENTERS OFFICE

9.) _____

FREEDOMS / RESTRICTIONS

10.) _____

11.) _____

12.) _____

13.) _____

INCOME TAX

14.) _____

CASES IN FEDERAL COURT

15.) _____

IF PRESIDENT DIES OR RESIGNS

16.) _____

CONGRESSIONAL PAY

17.) _____

READING: The Amendment Process

We have a living Constitution. Men wrote it in 1787, and we still use it today. These men were intelligent. "The U.S. will change in the future," they thought. "We must find a way to let the Constitution change, too." And they did.

They put in the amendment process. This process is important. Amendments can change or add rights and restrictions to the Constitution. An amendment can change part of an article in the Constitution or another amendment.

We have 27 amendments to the Constitution. Some deal with voting and elections. Others deal with freedoms or restrictions. Some deal with the President, or income tax, or cases in federal courts. They are all now the law of the United States.

Two–thirds (⅔) of the Congress or of the state legislatures must agree on an idea for an amendment. If three–fourths (¾) of the states ratify the amendment, it becomes part of the Constitution.

Using the Reading

C. Write questions using these words. Answer your questions. The first one is done for you as an example.

1. How / change / Constitution?

   Q. How can we change the Constitution?

   A. By amendment.

2. Who / must agree / idea / amendment?

   _____

   _____

   _____

   _____

3. How many / states / ratify / amendment?

   _____

   _____

   _____

   _____

4. Why / we / amend / Constitution?

   _____

   _____

   _____

   _____

REVIEW

Question	Answer
1. How many amendments does the Constitution have?	• 27
2. There are four amendments to the Constitution about who can vote. Describe <u>one</u> of them.	• citizens 18 years or older can vote • women can vote • black people can vote • you do not have to pay a tax to vote
3. How old do citizens have to be to vote for president?	• 18 years or older
4. If the president can no longer serve, who becomes president?	• the vice president
5. If the president and vice president can no longer serve, who becomes president?	• Speaker of the House

LESSON 13

EXECUTIVE BRANCH— PRESIDENT AND VICE PRESIDENT

OBJECTIVES

- Identify the powers of the executive branch
- Identify the qualifications of the president and vice president

PRE–READING

Oral

Discuss these questions with the class:

Who is the **president** of the U.S. **today**?

Who is the **vice president** of the U.S. **today**?

Tell the class about the leader of your country:

Is your leader a "president"?

If not, what do you call your leader?

What is the leader's name?

Can all adult citizens vote for the leader?

Listen to your classmates. Put the information about their countries in the chart below:

COUNTRY	LEADER	NAME	ADULTS CAN VOTE	
			YES	NO
U.S.	President		✔	

Here are pictures of two famous presidents.

George Washington

Abraham Lincoln

Vocabulary

Read the following words and definitions.

V.P.—vice president

(to) **veto**—to say "no"

(to) **approve**—to say "yes" or "okay"

(to) **appoint**—to choose

(to) **advise**—to give help and information

(to) **pardon**—to forgive a person for a federal crime; to give amnesty

soldiers—people in the army, navy, and air force

U.S. **foreign policy**—the way the U.S. government plans to act with other countries of the world

Written

Use the vocabulary above to unscramble the following words:

1. tevo _____

2. paveorp _____

3. savedi _____

4. toppina _____

Put three of these four words into the following sentences.

1. The Senate can _____ treaties.

2. The president needs help. The vice president can _____ her or him.

3. I want to be a judge. Do you think the president will _____ me?

INFORMATION: Duties of the President and Vice President

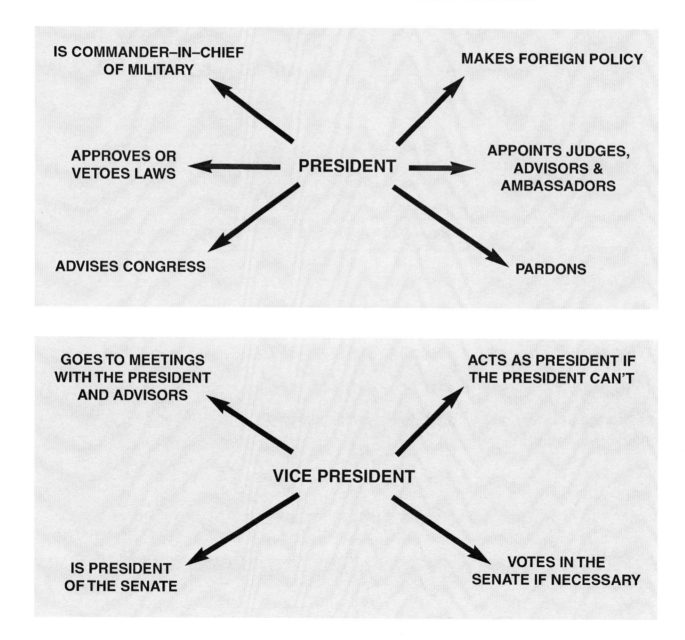

68   **For the People**

Using the Information

A. Look at the vocabulary and the information on the previous pages. Read the following sentences. The president can do three of these things. Check the three correct sentences.

The president ...

_____ 1. makes plans for foreign policy.

_____ 2. appoints people to the Supreme Court.

_____ 3. writes taxes for states.

_____ 4. votes in the Senate.

_____ 5. sends soldiers to war.

B. Form a small group. Talk about the activities of the president and the V.P. of the U.S.

What did they do this past week?

Did they go to another state or country?

Did they meet important people?

Make a list of all the things you remember. Share the information with the class.

READING: Qualifications of the President and Vice President

Do you want to be president? You must be born in the United States. You must live in the U.S. for 14 years or more. You must also be 35 years old or more. You can be president for a term of **4 years**. You can be elected again for **another 4 years** or one more term.

If the president dies, or resigns, or can't work, the vice president becomes president. So, the qualifications for vice president are the same as for the president.

The president and vice president are elected in November. They are sworn in (become president and vice president) on January 20 the next year.

Using the Reading

C. Look at the Reading. The lists below show the qualifications for president and vice president. Fill in the missing information.

PRESIDENT

1) __35__ + years old

2) be born _____

3) live in the U.S. for _____ years

4) only _____ elected terms

VICE PRESIDENT

5) _____+ years old

6) be born _____

7) live in the U.S. for _____ years

REVIEW

Question	**Answer**
1. Who is president of the United States today?	• Barack Obama *(This answer may change.)*
2. Who is the vice president of the United States today?	• Joe Biden *(This answer may change.)*
3. Who is in charge of the executive branch?	• the president
4. We elect a president for how many years?	• 4 years
5. Who is commander–in–chief of the U.S. military?	• the president
6. Who signs bills into law?	• the president
7. Who vetoes bills?	• the president
8. Who becomes president if the president dies?	• vice president

LESSON 14

EXECUTIVE BRANCH—
THE CABINET

OBJECTIVES

- Explain the role of the Cabinet
- Match executive departments with their responsibilities

PRE–READING

Oral

Look at the sequence of pictures. What do you think is happening?

Written

Read the following sentences. Each sentence tells about one of the pictures on page 71. Put the number of the picture next to the correct sentence.

_____ a) The president meets with the Cabinet. They talk about a problem. The Cabinet gives advice to the President.

_____ b) The president listens to Cabinet members with different ideas. One wants to build new apartments. The other member says it is too expensive.

_____ c) The president makes a decision and the Cabinet members agree.

_____ d) The president thinks about the problem.

Vocabulary

Read the following words and definitions.

The **Cabinet** is a group of advisors to the president. They are in charge of the executive departments.

We call most Cabinet members "**Secretary**." For example, Thomas Jefferson was the first Secretary of State. The State Department advises the president about foreign policy.

The head of the Justice Department is the **Attorney General**.

A **veteran** is a man or woman who was a soldier.

Juan needs money for college. He asks for **financial aid**.

Hilda is looking for some information. She goes to the library to do some **research**.

It is a very hot summer. We need to save water. We practice water **conservation**. We use water carefully.

We get a car **inspection** every year. We take our cars to a service station. A mechanic checks the car. He looks at the lights, brakes, and tires.

INFORMATION: The Cabinet

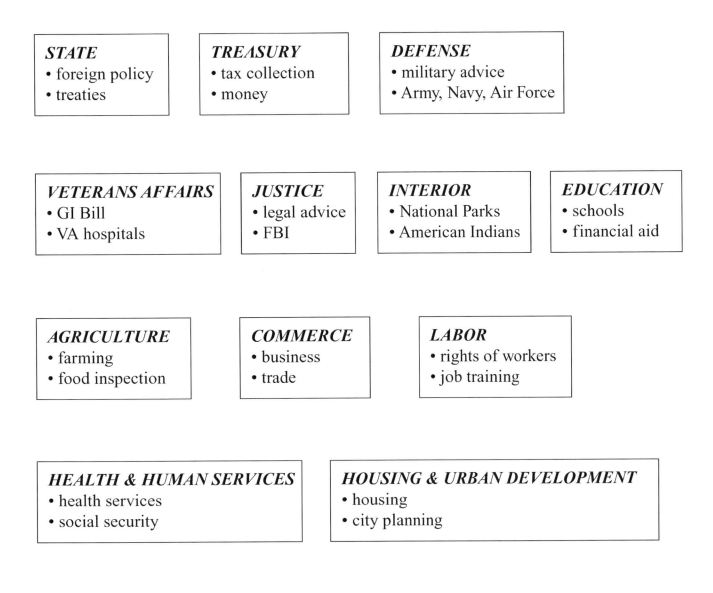

STATE
- foreign policy
- treaties

TREASURY
- tax collection
- money

DEFENSE
- military advice
- Army, Navy, Air Force

VETERANS AFFAIRS
- GI Bill
- VA hospitals

JUSTICE
- legal advice
- FBI

INTERIOR
- National Parks
- American Indians

EDUCATION
- schools
- financial aid

AGRICULTURE
- farming
- food inspection

COMMERCE
- business
- trade

LABOR
- rights of workers
- job training

HEALTH & HUMAN SERVICES
- health services
- social security

HOUSING & URBAN DEVELOPMENT
- housing
- city planning

TRANSPORTATION
- travel safety
- road, air, and train travel

ENERGY
- energy research
- energy conservation

HOMELAND SECURITY
- protect U.S.
- USCIS

Using the Information

A. Match the Cabinet department on the left with its responsibility on the right. Put the correct letter on the line.

_____ 1. Education   a) takes tax money from our paychecks

_____ 2. Health & Human Services b) helps train people for employment

_____ 3. Treasury   c) plans for special classes

_____ 4. Homeland Security   d) helps build low–cost housing

_____ 5. Labor   e) gives green cards

_____ 6. Housing & Urban Development f) gives Social Security cards

B. Play the game "Who Am I?" One student is a Cabinet member. The other students asks "yes/no" questions about his/her responsibilities. Try to guess the Cabinet member.

Example: Do you help farmers?

READING: The Cabinet and the President

There are 15 **executive departments (branches)** in our government. The heads of the executive departments are Cabinet members. The president appoints the members to the Cabinet. The president has weekly meetings with the Cabinet. They discuss problems. The Cabinet members **advise the president**.

Using the Reading

C. Read the following answers. Write a question for the answer. Use the information from the reading.

Example: Question: *Who advises the president*   ?
Answer: Cabinet members

1. _____?
Answer: 15

2. _____?
Answer: the president

3. _____?
Answer: problems

REVIEW

Question	**Answer**
1. What are <u>two</u> Cabinet level positions?	Secretary of: • Agriculture • Commerce • Defense • Education • Energy • Health and Human Services • Homeland Security • Housing and Urban Development • Interior • Labor • State • Transportation • Treasury • Veterans Affairs • Attorney General
2. What does the Cabinet do?	• Advises the president

LEGISLATIVE BRANCH— CONGRESS

OBJECTIVES

- Identify the two parts of Congress
- State the responsibilities of Congress

PRE–READING

Oral

Look at the picture of the U.S. Capitol in Washington, D.C.

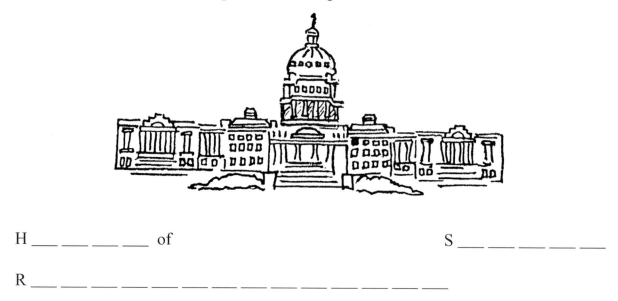

H ___ ___ ___ ___ of   S ___ ___ ___ ___ ___

R ___ ___ ___ ___ ___ ___ ___ ___ ___ ___ ___ ___ ___

Discuss these questions with your partner.

1. What city is the capital of the U.S.?

2. What is the capital of your country?

3. The U.S. Congress has two parts. What do we call them?

4. Does your country have a Congress?

Vocabulary

Read the following words and definitions.

(to) **declare war**—to tell the people "our country will fight"

authorization—legal permission or okay

title of nobility—an upper–class name ("king," "queen," "lord," etc.)

(to) **maintain**—to support with money

exports—things the U.S. sells to other countries

Written

Scan the sentences below. Then look at the following chart. Find the answers quickly. Circle **Y** (yes) or **N** (no).

1. Congress can declare war.   Y   N

2. Congress can give a title of nobility.   Y   N

3. Congress can maintain an army.   Y   N

4. Congress can make laws about marriage.   Y   N

INFORMATION: **Duties of the Congress**

Congress is made up of the **House of Representatives** and the **Senate**. They meet in the **U.S. Capitol Building**. The Constitution lists some duties for both the House of Representatives and the Senate. The Constitution also lists some things Congress cannot do. Read the chart below.

CONGRESS CAN	CONGRESS CANNOT
• make laws about trade • **maintain army, navy, air force** • **declare war** • make laws about taxes • establish U.S. Post Office • **make treaties** • borrow money • **print money**	• put a tax on exports • give title of nobility • use tax money without authorization • take away the right to a trial • make laws about marriage, driver's licenses, police, etc. (These are done by the states.)

Using the Information

A. Read the following sentences. Write "yes" next to the sentences about things Congress can do. Write "no" next to the sentences about things Congress cannot do.

_____ 1. say a person cannot have a trial in court

_____ 2. make new laws

_____ 3. send the army to war

_____ 4. say if a person can be a citizen

_____ 5. put a tax on things the U.S. sells to other countries

_____ 6. say a person is the King of America

_____ 7. maintain a police force

B. Form a small group. The Constitution lists some things Congress cannot do. The writers of the Constitution had a reason for this list. What do you think the reasons are? Discuss them with your group. Write your answers and share them with the class.

Example: Congress cannot give titles of nobility. Why not?

Because the writers wanted all Americans to be equal. They did not want anyone to become king or queen.

1. Congress cannot take away the right to a trial. Why not?

_____

_____

2. Congress cannot make laws about marriage. Why not?

_____

_____

_____

3. Congress cannot use tax money without authorization. Why not?

_____

_____

_____

READING: The Congress

The citizens of the United States elect a new Congress every two years, with the election of new senators and representatives. A **representative serves for 2 years**; a **senator for 6**. They **meet in the U.S. Capitol Building** to make **federal laws** for our country. There are **100 senators** and **435 representatives**. The time they meet to make laws is called a session.

Using the Reading

C. Use the words below to write questions. Then answer the questions.

1. When / new Congress / begin?

_____

_____

_____

2. What / we call / meeting / Congress?

_____

_____

_____

3. Where / Congress / meet?

_____

_____

_____

REVIEW

Question	**Answer**
1. What are the <u>two</u> parts of the U.S. Congress?	• Senate and House of Representatives
2. We elect a U.S. senator for how many years?	• six (6)
3. We elect a representative for how many years?	• two (2)
4. How many U.S. senators are there?	• 100
5. Who is <u>one</u> of your U.S. senators?	• _____
6. Name your U.S. representative.	• _____
7. Under our Constitution, some powers belong to the federal government. What is <u>one</u> power?	• prints money • declares war • maintains army, navy, and air force • makes treaties

LESSON 16

LEGISLATIVE BRANCH—
THE HOUSE OF REPRESENTATIVES

OBJECTIVES

- Explain duties of the House of Representatives
- Identify the qualifications of a representative

PRE–READING

Oral

Look at the map of the U.S. The map shows you the number of representatives for some states.

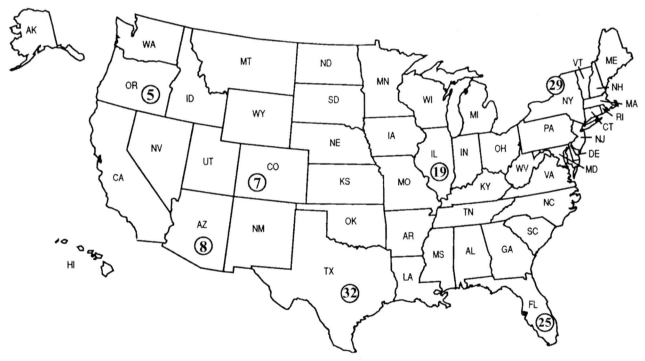

Discuss these questions with your partner.

1. Does every state have the same number of representatives?

2. How many representatives does your state have?

3. Do you know the name of your representative? Where can you find his/her name?

4. Does your country have representatives? How many?

Vocabulary

Complete the crossword puzzle. Use these words:

House	impeach	district	representative
represent	officials	budget	bill	propose

ACROSS

2 A member of the House of Representatives is a _ _ _ _ _ _ _ _ _ _ _ _ _ _ _ _ _ _.

5 A short form for House of Representatives is to say the _ _ _ _ _ _.

6 An idea for a new law is a _ _ _ _.

7 The voters elect officials. The officials _ _ _ _ _ _ _ _ _ the people.

8 If an official does something unconstitutional, the House can _ _ _ _ _ _ _ the official. The House tells the country the official did something wrong.

DOWN

1 People with important jobs in the government are called _ _ _ _ _ _ _ _ _.

3 To give an idea for the first time or to suggest an idea is to _ _ _ _ _ _ _ an idea.

4 An area in a city or state is a _ _ _ _ _ _ _ _.

6 A plan for spending money is a _ _ _ _ _ _.

INFORMATION: Members of the House of Representatives

There are **435 voting members** in the House of Representatives.

QUALIFICATIONS	REPRESENTS	SPECIAL DUTIES
Age: 25+ years U.S. citizen: 7+ years Live: in state Term: 2 years Limit: None	IOWA • Des Moines **1 district**	• impeach officials • propose bills on budget or taxes

Using the Information

A. Choose a partner. Student A reads sentences 1–3. Every sentence has a mistake in it. Student B looks at the chart and tries to repeat the sentence with the correct information. Switch roles for sentences 4–6. Student B reads and Student A corrects.

Example: A) A representative must be 35 or older.

B) No. A representative must be 25 or older.

1. A) A representative represents two states.

   B) _____

2. A) There are 455 members in the House.

   B) _____

3. A) Only the Senate can propose tax bills.

   B) _____

4. B) The term for a representative is 4 years.

   A) _____

5. B) Representatives must be citizens for 14 years.

   A) _____

6. B) Representatives can appoint officials.

   A) _____

B. Now read the same sentences again. Circle the mistake. Write the correction under the circled mistake.

Example: 1. A) A representative represents two states.

B) _____

READING: The Number of Representatives

There are **435 voting representatives** in the House. **The number for each state is based on population.** States with large populations, like California and Texas, have many representatives. Alaska and Delaware have only 1. In the year 2008, there was an average of about one representative for every 647,000 people. States with many representatives have more power in the House than states with only a few representatives.

Some states have many districts. The number of districts is equal to the number of representatives. The citizens of a district vote directly for their representative. Representatives listen to the needs of the people in their districts and their states.

The leader of the House of Representatives is called the Speaker. **He or she becomes President of the United States** if both the president and vice president cannot serve. Representative **Nancy Pelosi** is currently the Speaker of the House.

Using the Reading

C. Look at the maps of five different states. The number below the map tells us the population of that state in 2008. How many representatives did each state have? Write the number on the line below the population. Use these numbers:

1   2   13   11   53

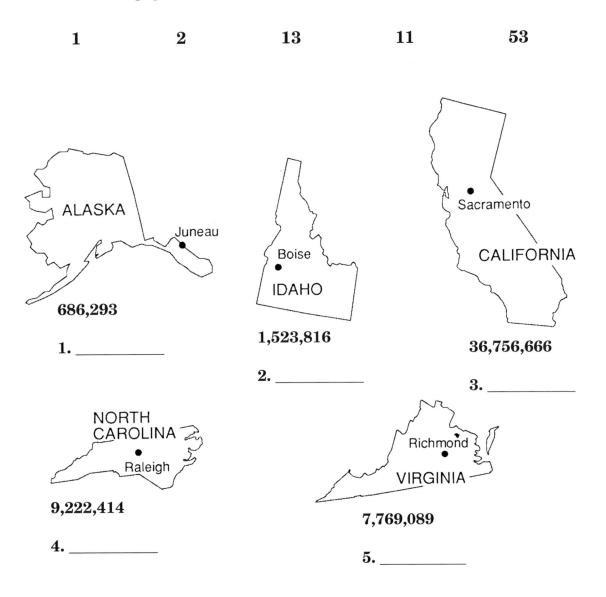

ALASKA Juneau

686,293

1. _____

Boise **IDAHO**

1,523,816

2. _____

Sacramento **CALIFORNIA**

36,756,666

3. _____

NORTH CAROLINA Raleigh

9,222,414

4. _____

Richmond VIRGINIA

7,769,089

5. _____

REVIEW

Question	**Answer**
1. The House of Representatives has how many voting members?	• 435
2. We elect a representative for how many years?	• Two (2)
3. Who becomes president if the president and vice president cannot serve?	• The Speaker of the House
4. Name your U.S. Representative.	• _____
5. Why do some states have more representatives than others?	• because of population • because they have more people
6. What is the name of the Speaker of the House of Representatives now?	• Nancy Pelosi *(This answer may change.)*

LEGISLATIVE BRANCH— THE SENATE

OBJECTIVES

- Explain the duties of the Senate
- Identify the qualifications of a senator

PRE–READING

Oral

Look at the map of the U.S. **Every state has two senators. They represent all the people of the entire state.**

Work with a partner. Discuss these questions.

1. How many senators work in the U.S. Congress?

2. Does every state have equal power in the Senate?

3. Do you know the names of your U.S. senators? Where can you find their names?

4. Does your or your family's country have senators? How many?

Vocabulary

Read the following words and definitions.

(to) **try** a public official—The Senate will decide if an official really did something unconstitutional (against the Constitution).

(to) **remove** from office—to tell an official to leave his/her job.

(to) **confirm appointments**—to approve people the President chooses for judges, ambassadors, and cabinet members.

majority—more than half; 51% or more.

Written

Read the vocabulary. Circle the word that does <u>not</u> belong.

Example: House   Senate   Congress   (President)
Answer: President (House, Senate, and Congress are words about the legislative branch.)

1. say yes	confirm	approve	say no
2. senators	ambassadors	cabinet	judges
3. remove	leave	stay	resign
4. one–fourth	majority	51%	three–fourths

INFORMATION: Members of the Senate

There are **100 members in the Senate**. Every state has two senators. They are elected for **6 years.**

QUALIFICATIONS	REPRESENTS	SPECIAL DUTIES
Age: 30+ years U.S. citizen: 9+ years Live: in state Term: 6 years Limit: None	Columbia • SOUTH CAROLINA entire state	• ratify/approve treaties • confirm appointments • try impeached officials

Using the Information

A. Work with a partner. Student A reads sentences 1–3. Student B answers **T** (true) or **F** (false).

STUDENT A	STUDENT B
1. A senator's term is 4 years.	T F
2. The Senate starts bills about taxes.	T F
3. Senators must be at least 30 years old.	T F

Switch roles. Student B reads sentences 4–6. Student A answers **T** or **F**.

STUDENT B	STUDENT A
4. There are 100 senators.	T F
5. Senators represent only one district.	T F
6. The Senate ratifies treaties.	T F

B. Three of the sentences above are false. Make them true. Rewrite them on the lines below.

_____

_____

_____

READING: The Number of Senators

There are **100** senators in the Senate. Each state elects two senators. They serve for **6 years**. The Senate is regarded as a more deliberative body than the House of Representatives. The Senate has several powers not granted to the House. The president cannot ratify treaties or make important appointments without the advice and consent of the Senate.

REVIEW

Question	Answer
1. How many U.S. senators are there?	•100
2. We elect a senator for how many years?	•Six (6)
3. Who is <u>one</u> of your state's senators?	• _____
	• _____
4. Who does a U.S. senator represent?	• the people of the entire state

JUDICIAL BRANCH—
THE SUPREME COURT

OBJECTIVE

- Explain the role of the Supreme Court

PRE–READING

Oral

Look at the picture of the Supreme Court below.

Discuss the court system in your country.

Does your country have a Supreme Court?

Does your country have an appeals process?

How does someone become a judge in your country?

Does your country have juries?

Vocabulary

Match the words on the left with the definition on the right. Put the correct letter on the line.

_____ 1. **justice**　　　　　a) highest court in the U.S.

_____ 2. **jury**　　　　　b) decision: you did nothing wrong

_____ 3. **judicial branch**　　　c) court system of the U.S. government

_____ 4. **Supreme Court**　　　d) a judge on the Supreme Court

_____ 5. **innocent**　　　　e) decision: you did something wrong

_____ 6. **guilty**　　　　f) people who make a decision in a case

INFORMATION: The Supreme Court

The following picture shows the Supreme Court's bench. The Supreme Court is in Washington, D.C. The **nine justices** sit and listen to important cases.

- **Nine justices**
- **Justices choose the cases to hear**
- **Supreme Court decisions are final**
- **Justices can say a state or federal law is unconstitutional**

Using the Information

A. Read the following sentences. Are they true or false? Circle **T** or **F**.

1. You can appeal a Supreme Court decision.   T   F

2. The Supreme Court hears all appellate cases.   T   F

3. There is a jury and nine justices on the Supreme Court.   T   F

4. The Supreme Court listens only to cases about federal laws.   T   F

5. The Supreme Court is in Washington, D.C.   T   F

READING: Supreme Court Justices

Supreme Court justices have an important job. They must **interpret and explain the laws** of the United States. **They must decide if a law goes against the Constitution**. Their decisions can affect all U.S. citizens. One of the **nine justices** is the chief justice. Currently that is **John Roberts**.

The president nominates someone to be a justice. The Senate must approve the president's choice. Supreme Court justices have the position until they die or retire.

Using the Reading

B. Answer the following questions:

1. Who chooses a Supreme Court justice?

2. What is the job of the Supreme Court justices?

3. How many chief justices are on the Supreme Court?

4. If there is a new president, do all the Supreme Court justices change?

REVIEW

Question	Answer
1. What is the highest court in the United States?	• The Supreme Court
2. What does the judicial branch do?	• reviews laws • explains laws • decides if a law goes against the Constitution
3. How many justices are on the Supreme Court?	• nine (9)
4. Who is the Chief Justice of the Supreme Court?	• John Roberts

LESSON 19

STATE AND LOCAL GOVERNMENT— STRUCTURE AND RESPONSIBILITIES

OBJECTIVES

- Identify the structure of state and local governments
- Identify state and local leaders

PRE–READING

Oral

Look at the charts below. Discuss what is the same or different about them with a partner.

Federal Government	State Government	Local Government
President	Governor	Mayor / City Manager
Vice President	Lieutenant Governor	
(Advisors)	(Advisors)	
Congress	Legislature	City Council / Commission
Supreme Court	State Supreme Court	Local Courts

Vocabulary

Read the following words and definitions.

assembly—the name for the House of Representatives in some state legislatures

governor—the chief executive in a state

lieutenant governor—the assistant governor, the second–in–command in the state executive branch

National Guard—the military force of a state; the governor is the chief

petition—a voter (or group of voters) can write a paper (a petition) to explain a problem, ask for a new law, or change a law. A petition must have the signatures of many citizens before a state legislature will review it.

READING: State and Local Government Responsibilities

The U.S. Constitution says: If the federal government does not have certain powers in the Constitution, then the states or the people do. For example, the states have responsibility for the education system and driver's and marriage licenses. The states can build roads in their state and make rules for trade in their states. State governments can collect taxes, establish courts, and make laws for their state. One important point to remember: No state law can go against the U.S. Constitution!

Local governments are different from state and federal governments because they do not have constitutions. Sometimes people elect a mayor as the head of their local (city) government. Sometimes it is a city council or a commission. Local governments are closest to the people. They hire policeman and firemen. They have family and traffic courts. They have responsibility for collecting the garbage and collecting taxes on houses.

Using the Reading

A. Use the information in the paragraphs to fill in the charts below. List four responsibilities for each side.

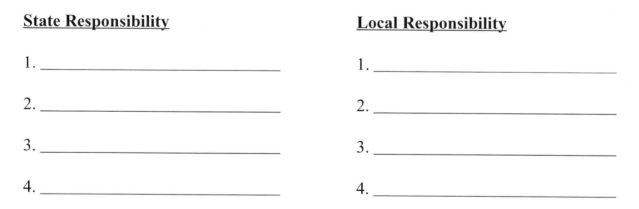

State Responsibility

1. _____

2. _____

3. _____

4. _____

Local Responsibility

1. _____

2. _____

3. _____

4. _____

B. Are the following sentences true or false? Circle **T** or **F**. Correct all the false sentences.

1. A petition is an example of direct democracy.   T   F

2. Many citizens think they can change federal laws easily.   T   F

3. Sometimes, citizens of a state vote to make changes in state laws.   T   F

4. Petitions can ask only for new laws.   T   F

C. Write the answers to the following questions.

1. What kind of local government do you have?

_____

2. Does your local government have a constitution?

_____

3. Have you ever been to a local court?

_____

REVIEW

Question

1. What is the capital of your state?

2. Who is the current governor of your state?

3. Under our Constitution, some powers belong to the state. What is <u>one</u> power of the state?

Answer

• _____

• _____

• provide schooling and education
• issue driver's or marriage licenses
• build roads
• approve zoning

THE GROWTH OF THE
UNITED STATES (1800–1900)

OBJECTIVES

- Identify the territorial growth in the U.S.
- Explain reasons for expanding west

PRE–READING

Oral

Form a small group. Talk about the American West. Make a list of everything you know. These pictures will give you some ideas to start. Later, share your group's list with the other groups.

Vocabulary

Read the following words and definitions.

annexation—taking control of land from another country

cattle—cows

cession—when one country gives land to another country

destiny—fate; something that will definitely happen

(to) **expand**—to become larger; to grow

farmland—land for farming

Written

Scan the paragraph below. Are the following sentences true (T) or false (F)? Circle **T** or **F**.

1. Americans wanted to use the Mississippi River.	T	F
2. The land in the West was good for cattle.	T	F
3. People wanted to build factories in the West.	T	F
4. Gold was discovered in Texas.	T	F
5. The U.S. expanded in the 1800s.	T	F

There are many reasons the U.S. expanded in the 1800s. Many Americans wanted farmland in the West. They wanted land to raise cattle. Americans wanted to transport goods on the Mississippi River, **the longest river in the U.S.,** to New Orleans. Some people were tired of factory work. They wanted to go west. Others went west because they heard there was gold in California and Alaska. The U.S. government wanted to control all the land from the Atlantic Ocean to the Pacific Ocean. They wanted all foreign countries to give up their land in the U.S.

INFORMATION: The Nation Grows

This map shows the new territories of the U.S. in the 1800s. Sometimes, the government bought the land. Sometimes, the U.S. fought a war for the land. Other times, the U.S. signed a treaty for the land. The U.S. got the land from France, Spain, Mexico, England, and Russia, as shown by the different patterns on the map.

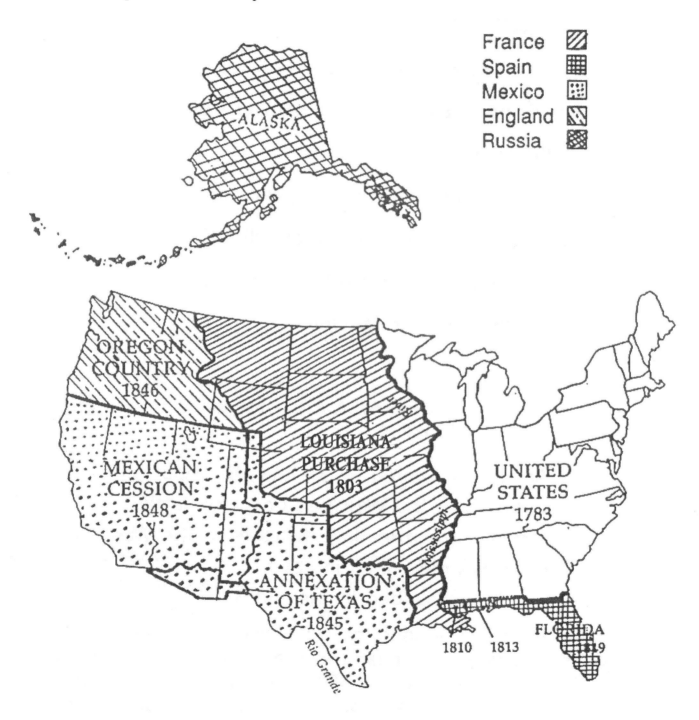

Using the Information

A. The map on page 100 shows the U.S. and the new territories in the 1800s. Find a current map of the U.S. with the 50 states. Put the following states in the correct boxes.

California   Nebraska   Arizona   Washington   Idaho   Texas

Oklahoma   Oregon   Utah   Missouri   Kansas   South Dakota

LOUISIANA PURCHASE

1. _____

2. _____

3. _____

4. _____

5. _____

OREGON COUNTRY

1. _____

2. _____

3. _____

MEXICAN CESSION

1. _____

2. _____

3. _____

ANNEXATION OF TEXAS

1. _____

B. Look at the timeline on the following page. Answer the following questions.

1. What land did the U.S. buy from France? When?

   _____

2. What land did the U.S. buy from Spain? When?

   _____

3. In what year did the U.S. fight England?

   _____

4. When was the Mexican–American War?

   _____

5. When was the Civil War?

_____

6. In what year did Texas become a state?

_____

1800

1803	**Louisiana Purchase**
1812	**War with England**
1819	**U.S. bought Florida**
1845	**Texas became a state**
1846–1848	**Mexican–American War**
1861–1865	**U.S. Civil War**
1867	**U.S. bought Alaska**
1898	**Spanish–American War**

1900

READING: Expansion West

There were many changes in the 1800s. The country became stronger and more important. There were more people in the country. Americans believed the country should reach the Pacific Ocean.

There are many reasons the U.S. expanded in the 1800s. Many Americans wanted farmland in the West. They wanted land to raise cattle. Americans wanted to transport goods on the Mississippi River to New Orleans. Some people were tired of factory work. They wanted to go west. Others went west because they heard there was gold in California and Alaska. The U.S. government wanted to control all the land from the Atlantic Ocean to the Pacific Ocean. They wanted all foreign countries to give up their land in the U.S.

The move west was good for the settlers, but there were many problems, too. There was a lot of fighting between the settlers and the Indians. The U.S. government and the Native Americans signed many treaties. Native Americans lost most of their land to farmers and the railroad.

The U.S. got the new territories from different countries. Sometimes, the U.S. bought the land. The U.S. bought the Louisiana Territory from France, Florida from Spain, and Alaska from Russia.

Sometimes, the U.S. fought a war for land. The U.S. fought Mexico for Texas and the Southwest. Other times, the U.S. signed a treaty for land.

Using the Reading

C. Complete the outline below. You can find the information in the Reading.

I. Why American people wanted to go west

A. _____

B. _____

C. _____

D. _____

II. Land the U.S. bought

    A. _____

    B. _____

    C. _____

III. Land the U.S. fought for

    A. _____

    B. _____

REVIEW

Question	Answer
1. What territory did the United States buy from France in 1803?	• the Louisiana Territory
2. Name <u>one</u> war fought by the United States in the 1800s.	• War of 1812 • Civil War • Mexican–American War • Spanish–American War
3. Name the U.S. war between the North and the South.	• The Civil War • the war between the states
4. Name <u>one</u> of the longest rivers in the United States.	• Mississippi

LESSON 21

BEFORE THE CIVIL WAR

OBJECTIVE

- Explain the causes of the American Civil War

PRE–READING

Map Skills

Look at the map of the U.S. from 1850.

Use the key to find the free states and the slave states. Write the names of the states in the correct box.

FREE		SLAVE	
Maine		*Delaware*	

Oral
Form a small group. Discuss these questions.

1. Where were most of the slave states?

2. Where were most of the free states?

3. There were many differences between the northern and the southern states. What is one difference you see on the map?

4. The U.S. had a civil war between 1861 and 1865. Was there ever a civil war in your country?

5. How is a civil war different from other wars?

Vocabulary

Use the new words to complete the crossword puzzle. You can use a dictionary to help you.

plantation	abolish	obey	Union
abolitionists	secede	divide	economy

ACROSS

1 a large farm, usually in the South

3 people against slavery; they wanted to stop slavery

6 a group of states joined together

7 everything related to money (dollars, trade, industry, etc.)

8 to separate or split

DOWN

2 to stop; to put an end to something

4 to do what the law says; to follow the rules

5 when a state separates from the country

INFORMATION: Differences Between the North and the South

(I) Ways to make money

North	South
Industry: The people made money in industry. There were many factories. The factories made many goods.	*Agriculture:* The people made money on large plantations. They grew cotton, tobacco, and rice. The plantations needed slaves to do the work.

(II) Ideas about tariffs

North	South
U.S. industry was young. Goods made in the U.S. were more expensive than goods from Europe. The North wanted tariffs on goods from other countries. They wanted people to buy U.S. goods.	The South did not have factories. They sold their agricultural products to Europe and the North. They wanted to buy cheaper goods from Europe. They did not want tariffs to raise the prices of foreign goods.

(III) Number of Representatives

North	South
There were more people in the North. They had more representatives. The North had more power in the House of Representatives.	There were fewer people in the South. They had fewer representatives. The South had less power in the House of Representatives.

(IV) Ideas about the federal government

North	South
The North believed in a federal government. They said all states must obey all federal laws. They said the country was a "Union," not individual states. The country could not divide.	The South believed in strong state governments. They said states did not have to obey federal laws. They said the country was "an agreement among the states." States could secede. This is called **states' rights**.

Using the Information

A. Read the following sentences. Decide if they tell you about the North or the South. Write the words <u>North</u> or <u>South</u> on the lines. Look at the boxes again if you need help.

1. The _____ had more power in the House of Representatives.

2. The _____ believed the nation was more important than the states.

3. The _____ believed the rights of the states were more important.

4. The _____ did not like tariffs on foreign goods.

5. The _____ had many factories.

6. The _____ had less power in the House of Representatives.

7. The _____ had cotton plantations.

8. The _____ wanted tariffs on foreign goods.

B. Work with a partner. Pretend you are living in the U.S. in the 1850s. One person will be from the South. The other person will be from the North.

Choose one of the following pairs. What do you think these people would talk about? Make up a conversation. Then share your conversation with the class.

- southern slave and northern factory worker

- plantation owner and factory owner

- representative from the South and representative from the North

- poor woman from the South and poor woman from the North

READING: The Problem of Slavery

There were many differences between the North and the South. One important difference was slavery. Since the early days of the U.S., **groups of black people were taken from Africa and sold as slaves**. In the 1800s, the South needed many people to work on the plantations. Plantation owners bought slaves to do this work. Slavery was important to the economy of the South. Some people in the North did not like slavery. They said slavery took away individual freedoms. These people wanted to abolish slavery. They were called abolitionists.

The problem of slavery grew with the country. The North wanted new states to be free states (without slavery). The South wanted new states to be slave states (with slavery). In 1820 there were 11 free states and 11 slave states. The North and the South had the same number of senators in Congress. Then Missouri asked to become a state. If Missouri became a free state, the North would have more senators. The South did not want the North to have more senators and more representatives. The men in Congress had many discussions about this problem. It was very difficult for both sides to agree. Finally, they compromised. The Missouri Compromise made Missouri a slave state and Maine a free state.

The problems did not stop with the Missouri Compromise. In 1850, California asked to become a free state. There were 15 slave states and 15 free states at that time. Congress had to make a new compromise. In the Compromise of 1850, California became a free state, but the other parts of the Mexican Cession could be slave states or free states. The people in the new states would vote and decide.

There were problems in other areas, too. Slave owners and abolitionists tried to settle the lands of Kansas and Nebraska. The slave owners wanted the people to vote for Kansas and Nebraska to be slave states. The abolitionists wanted people to vote to be free. Sometimes the two sides fought. The problems were growing.

Using the Reading

C. Use these words to write questions. You have to add some words. Later, ask your partner to answer the questions.

1. Why / slavery / important / South?

_____

_____

2. What / abolitionists / want?

_____

_____

3. How many / slave states / U.S. / have / in 1820?

_____

_____

4. What / Missouri Compromise?

_____

_____

5. What / Compromise of 1850?

_____

_____

D. Read the following sentences and questions. Circle the letter of the sentence or question with the same meaning

1. What were the causes of the Civil War?

   a) What happened after the Civil War?

   b) What problems started the Civil War?

   c) What happened during the Civil War?

2. The North wanted new states to be free states.

   a) The North did not want taxes in the new states.

   b) The North did not want slaves in the new states.

   c) The North wanted the new states to have factories.

3. The abolitionists wanted to put an end to slavery.

   a) The abolitionists wanted to stop slavery.

   b) The abolitionists wanted to kill slaves.

   c) The abolitionists wanted to sell slaves.

4. The South had less power in Congress.

   a) The South had fewer representatives in Congress than the North after 1850.

   b) The South did not agree with all the federal laws.

   c) The South wanted weaker state governments.

REVIEW

Question	**Answer**
1. Name <u>one</u> problem that led to the Civil War.	• slavery • economic reasons • states' rights

THE CIVIL WAR (1861–1865)

OBJECTIVES

- Explain the Emancipation Proclamation
- Explain why Lincoln was an important president

PRE–READING

Oral

Look at the six pictures below. These pictures tell us something about a famous American president. Do you know his name? What else do you know about him?

1.

2.

3.

4.

5.

FEBRUARY						
S	M	T	W	TH	F	S
1	2	3	4	5	6	7
8	9	10	11	12	13	14
15	⑯	17	18	19	20	21
22	23	24	25	26	27	28

6.

Written

Read the six sentences below and look at the pictures on page 113. Put the number of the picture next to the correct sentence. Check your answers with the class.

___5___ a) The Lincoln Memorial is in Washington, D.C.

_____ b) He was born in a log cabin.

_____ c) Abraham Lincoln was a famous U.S. president.

_____ d) We remember Lincoln on Presidents' Day. It is the third Monday in February.

_____ e) He was killed in 1865.

_____ f) He made many famous speeches.

Vocabulary

Write definitions for these terms.

supply line— _____

_____

advantages— _____

_____

(to) **assassinate—** _____

_____

goal— _____

_____

(to) **reunite—** _____

_____

(to) **surrender**—_____

_____

secede—_____

_____

INFORMATION: The American Civil War

Events: 1. Lincoln was elected president.

2. South Carolina seceded from the U.S.

3. Ten other states seceded.

4. Eleven southern states formed the Confederate States of America.

5. Confederates attacked a federal fort in South Carolina.

6. Union and Confederate Armies fought the Civil War 1861–1865.

7. Confederates surrendered in Virginia.

UNION	CONFEDERATE
Idea: Country cannot divide	*Idea:* States can secede; they had **states' rights**
Army Leader: Ulysses S. Grant	*Army Leaders:* Robert E. Lee, Stonewall Jackson
Advantages: • had more money • had larger population • had factories for weapons • had more railroads • controlled the navy	*Advantages:* • fought more battles in the South • had short supply lines • had some excellent leaders • believed they were better fighters • thought England and France would help

Using the Information

A. Look at the map on page 115. It shows some of the Confederate states. Use the map to complete the chart below. Write the names of the other Confederate states.

1. _Texas_
2. _Arkansas_
3. _____
4. _____
5. _____
6. _____

7. _____
8. _____
9. _____
10. _____
11. _____

B. In the Information you see many advantages for the North and the South. The war was long because both sides were very strong.

Form a small group. Discuss the following questions with your group. Share your group's answers with the class.

1. What do you think was the most important Union advantage?

2. What do you think was the most important Confederate advantage?

3. Why do you think the Union won the war?

READING: Abraham Lincoln

Abraham Lincoln was born in a log cabin in Kentucky. Later his family moved to Illinois. They were poor. He went to school for only one year. He learned by reading all the time. He studied hard and became a lawyer.

Abraham Lincoln was elected the 16th President of the U.S. in 1860. The people in the South did not like Lincoln because he was from the North. Lincoln did not want slavery in the new states. The South was afraid he would abolish slavery.

We remember Lincoln because he was a strong president during the Civil War. He believed the country should stay together. He said the Confederate States could not secede. His goal during the Civil War was to **save the Union**.

Lincoln was a great speaker. He is famous for the **Emancipation Proclamation**. In the Emancipation Proclamation, Lincoln **freed the slaves**. **He said all slaves in the Confederate States were free.** He said blacks could fight in the Union Army.

Lincoln's most famous speech was the Gettysburg Address. He made the speech in Gettysburg, Pennsylvania, in 1863. Lincoln told the people to remember these important words from the Declaration of Independence: "…all men are created equal…" He also said, "…a government of the people, by the people, for the people…" will stay together.

The Civil War ended in 1865. Lincoln was elected president again. He had great plans to reunite the country. But Lincoln did not live to reunite the country. He was assassinated five days after the election.

Using the Reading

C. Work with a partner. Student A reads sentences 1–3. Student B tells if they are true (**T**) or false (**F**).

STUDENT A	STUDENT B	
1. Lincoln's family had a lot of money.	T	F
2. Lincoln's goal was to save the Union.	T	F
3. Blacks could not fight in the Civil War.	T	F

Switch roles. Student B reads sentences 4–6. Student A tells if they are **T** or **F**.

STUDENT B	STUDENT A	
4. The South did not want Lincoln to be president.	T	F
5. Lincoln was elected president three times.	T	F
6. Lincoln believed the government was for white people only.	T	F

D. Four of the sentences in exercise C are false. Which ones? Rewrite the false sentences below. Make them true sentences.

_____

_____

_____

_____

_____

_____

_____

_____

REVIEW

Question	**Answer**
1. What did the Emancipation Proclamation do?	• freed the slaves • freed the slaves in the Confederate States
2. What was <u>one</u> important thing that Abraham Lincoln did?	• freed the slaves • saved the Union • led the U.S. during the Civil War

LESSON 23

THE GROWTH OF THE UNITED STATES (1900–2000)

OBJECTIVE

- Identify major events during the 1900s

PRE–READING

Oral

Form a small group. Discuss the following situations with your classmates.

What happens when…

- farms produce too much food or factories produce too many goods?
- people lose their jobs and buy everything on credit?
- homes lose their value, people cannot sell, and rents go up?

Do you think…

- the Great Depression came from World War I?
- World War II came from World War I?

Vocabulary

Use a dictionary. Write a definition for these words.

regulation— _____

_____

depression— _____

_____

credit— _____

_____

Nazi— _____

_____

axis— _____

_____

stocks— _____

_____

loan— _____

_____

veteran— _____

_____

atomic bomb— _____

_____

invasion— _____

_____

INFORMATION: The 1900s

Look at the highlights in the following timeline:

1900

1912	Woodrow Wilson elected president
1914	**World War I** begins in Europe
1916	Woodrow Wilson re–elected
1917–1919	The U.S. fights in **World War I**
1920	19th Amendment (women can vote)
1929–1939	The **Great Depression**
1941–1945	U.S. fights in **World War II**
1945	The **Cold War** starts
1950–1953	U.S. fights in the **Korean War**
1955	The modern **Civil Rights** era begins
1964–1973	U.S. fights in **Vietnam**
1989	The Berlin Wall falls
1991	U.S. fights in **Persian Gulf War**

2000

Using the Information

A. Read the following sentences. Using the Information on page 121, cirlce true (**T**) or false (**F**).

1. The U.S. fought many wars in the 1900s.   T   F

2. The Great Depression lasted 2 years.   T   F

3. The Cold War began in 1960.   T   F

4. The Civil Rights movement started in 1955.   T   F

READING : World War I , World War II, and the Cold War

In 1914 World War I began in Europe. **Woodrow Wilson was president** of the U.S. then. His policy was isolation. He wanted the U.S. to be neutral. In 1917 a German submarine attacked a U.S. trade ship, and the U.S. entered the war on the side of the Allies. The Germans surrendered on November 11, 1918. We celebrate **Veterans Day** as a national holiday on November 18.

There were many economic problems in the world after World War I. In the U.S. there was a great depression. Factories could not sell their goods; workers lost jobs; food prices started to decrease; there was not enough food; people bought less. **Franklin Roosevelt was elected president** in 1932. He promised to end the Depression. There were economic problems in Europe, too. France and England did not want to fight another war, but Germany and Italy fought against England and France. The U.S. Congress passed laws to keep America out of World War II. Then in December of 1941, the **Japanese** attacked the U.S. at Pearl Harbor in Hawaii, and America again joined the Allies and declared war. **General Dwight Eisenhower** led the war for the U.S. against Germany and Italy; General Douglas MacArthur led the war for the U.S. against Japan.

Many countries were destroyed in World War II. They were poor after the war. **Germany, Italy and Japan** were completely defeated. England and France lost most of their world power. The Soviet Union and the U.S. became the most powerful countries in the world. Both countries tried to persuade other countries to adopt their economic systems. The U.S. has a capitalistic or free market economy. The **Soviet Union has Communism**. Most of Eastern Europe was under **Communist** control. Most of Western Europe sided with the U.S. In 1989, the **Cold War** began to "thaw." Berliners tore down the Berlin Wall. It was the dividing line between East and West.

Using the Reading

B. Use these words to write questions. You have to add some words. Later, ask your partner to answer the questions.

1. What / countries / in / World War II?

   _____

2. Which / general / U.S. / World War II?

   _____

3. What / countries / powerful / after / World War II?

   _____

4. What / economic / system / U.S. / have?

   _____

5. What / people / lose / in the / Depression?

   _____

6. What / Cold War / mean?

   _____

REVIEW

Question	**Answer**
1. Name <u>one</u> war fought by the U.S. in the 1900s.	• World War I • World War II • Korean War • Vietnam War • Persian Gulf War
2. Who was president during World War I?	• Woodrow Wilson
3. Who was president during the Great Depression and World War II?	• Franklin Roosevelt
4. Who did the U.S. fight in World War II?	• Germany, Italy, and Japan
5. Before he was president, Eisenhower was a general. What war was he in?	• World War II
6. What is <u>one</u> national U.S. holiday?	• Veterans Day
7. During the Cold War, what was the main concern of the U.S.?	• Communism

THE UNITED STATES
AND CIVIL RIGHTS

OBJECTIVES

- Identify the main issues leading to the Civil Rights movement, and the results
- Identify Martin Luther King, Jr.

PRE-READING

Oral

Work with a partner. Discuss these questions.

Think about colonial America. The colonists did not like some laws and taxes from England. What did they do? How did they protest?

Think of a problem you have today. Maybe it is a problem about employment or about taxes or about insurance. What actions can you take?

Vocabulary

Match the words on the left with the definitions on the right. Put the correct letter on the line. You can use a dictionary for help.

_____1. **segregation**	a) a type of protest
_____2. **discrimination**	b) to treat unfairly
_____3. (to) **boycott**	c) no fighting, hitting, or shooting
_____4. **sit-in**	d) to separate by race
_____5. **nonviolent**	e) to refuse to have anything to do with
_____6. **integration**	f) equality

INFORMATION: The Civil Rights Movement

> *Problem:*
>
> Segregation of Blacks and Whites:
> - unequal schooling
> - Blacks had to sit in the back of buses
> - "White Only" restaurants, restrooms, etc.
>
> Discrimination and racism

Actions:	*Results:*
Nonviolent demonstrations: • sit–ins, boycotts • marches, speeches Martin Luther King, Jr., became a famous leader.	Civil Rights laws (1957, 1960, 1964, and 1968) • fair employment • Voting Rights Act of 1970 Supreme Court decisions: for example, *Brown v. Board of Education*

Using the Information

A. Read the three questions and the answer below. Choose the best question for the answer. Circle the correct letter.

Example: (a) What was a problem for Blacks?

b) Who sat in the back of buses?

c) What was an action during the Civil Rights movement?

Answer: Discrimination

(You circle a. "Discrimination" is the answer to "What was a problem for Blacks?")

1. a) What were some results of the Civil Rights movement?

b) What were some types of nonviolent demonstrations?

c) What were the names of famous Civil Rights leaders?

Answer: Boycotts, sit–ins, and marches.

2. a) Who was a leader of the Civil Rights movement?

   b) Who did not want civil rights?

   c) Who benefited from segregation?

   Answer: Martin Luther King, Jr.

3. a) What was a problem during the Civil Rights movement?

   b) What was a famous Supreme Court case for civil rights?

   c) What helped Blacks get better job situations and stopped voting discrimination?

   Answer: The Civil Rights laws of 1957, 1960, 1964, and 1968.

B. Divide the class into two groups. Have a debate about civil rights. One side believes segregation is a good thing. The other side believes integration is a good thing. The debate in the 1950s and 1960s focused on Blacks and Whites. Do you think Hispanic, Asian, and other groups should be included? Should there be separate schools, restaurants, restrooms, etc., for all these groups?

READING: Martin Luther King, Jr.

The **Civil Rights movement tried to end racial discrimination in the U.S.** In colonial days, **people were brought to the U.S. from Africa and sold as slaves. Abraham Lincoln freed the slaves.** Yet discrimination still existed.

The **Reverend Martin Luther King, Jr.**, was a famous leader of the **Civil Rights movement**. He believed Blacks could change the opinions of many Americans with nonviolent demonstrations. He wanted to stop segregation, but he did not want fighting or violence. One law said Blacks had to sit in the back of buses. This was not fair.

King helped plan a boycott of buses in Montgomery, Alabama. Blacks did not ride on the buses for more than one year. Finally, segregation on buses stopped. King also led nonviolent protests, demonstrations, sit–ins, and marches all over the U.S.

In January, we celebrate **Martin Luther King, Jr., Day**. It is a national holiday.

Using the Reading

C. Answer the following questions.

1. What methods did King use to change opinions of many Americans?

_____

_____

2. Why did he plan a bus boycott?

_____

_____

3. Was the Civil Rights movement successful? Name some results of the movement.

_____

_____

REVIEW

Question	**Answer**
1. What did Martin Luther King, Jr., do?	• fought for civil rights • worked for equality
2. What movement tried to end racial discrimination?	• the civil rights movement
3. What group of people were taken to America and sold as slaves?	• Africans • people from Africa
4. What was <u>one</u> thing that Abraham Lincoln did?	• freed the slaves
5. Name <u>one</u> national U.S. holiday.	• Martin Luther King, Jr., Day

THE UNITED STATES—
FROM THE ATLANTIC TO THE PACIFIC/
CANADA TO MEXICO

OBJECTIVES

- Identify the size of the U.S.
- Identify the border states

PRE–READING

Oral

Look at the map below.

Form a small group. Discuss these questions.

1. Which is the biggest border?

2. Which border gives the U.S. the most problems?

3. Why do you think that is?

4. How many miles do you think it is from the Atlantic to the Pacific?

Use the map on page 129 to fill in the names of states that border the United States on the North (Canadian border) and the South (Mexican border).

Northern Border	Southern Border

Vocabulary
Read the following words and definitions.

border—an edge between one county and another

reservation—an area of land where Indians live

rhythm—a pattern

extinguish—to put out

territory—land under control of the U.S.

READING: The Geography of the United States

The United States is a big country. It goes from the **Atlantic Ocean on the East** to the **Pacific Ocean on the West.** Canada has the longest border with the U. S. The states that border Canada are: **Maine, New Hampshire, Vermont, New York, Pennsylvania, Ohio, Michigan, Minnesota, North Dakota, Montana, Idaho, Washington** and **Alaska.** It is very big. Only four states share a border with Mexico. They are: **California, Arizona, New Mexico,** and **Texas.**

There are many rivers that run through the U.S. The **Mississippi River** starts on the Canadian border in Minnesota and runs through the entire country to the Gulf of Mexico in Louisiana. It is used to transport goods and people. The **Missouri** and the **Rio Grande** are also big rivers. The United States also has territories. **Puerto Rico, Guam, America Samoa** and the **Virgin Islands** in the Caribbean are U. S. territories.

Long before the European colonists came to the U.S., about 10,000 Native Americans (American Indians) lived here. They lived with the rhythm and spirit of nature. To the colonists, nature was a resource. The forests had timber. The beavers had pelts. The buffalo had meat and warm coats.

Even the Indians themselves were a resource. They were souls for the Jesuits, and the Dominicans, and the Puritans. There were wars between the Indians and the settlers. Now many Indians live on reservations. There are **Navajo, Hopi, Pueblo,** and **Apache** reservations in New Mexico and Arizona. The **Chippewas** and **Hurons** live mostly in the midwest. The **Seminoles** are in Florida, and the **Iroquois** nation is in the northeast. The Europeans tried to extinguish the Indians. They are still alive throughout the United States.

Using the Reading

A. Work with a partner. Student A reads sentences 1–3. Student B tells if they are true (**T**) or false (**F**).

STUDENT A	STUDENT B	
1. California borders Canada.	T	F
2. When the colonists came, there were no people in the U.S.	T	F
3. The Mississippi is a big river.	T	F

Switch roles. Student B reads sentences 4–6. Student A tells if they are **T** or **F**.

STUDENT B	STUDENT A	
4. The Chippewa Indians live in Minnesota and Michigan.	T	F
5. The U.S. is bigger than Mexico.	T	F
6. The Pacific Ocean is on the east coast of the U.S.	T	F

REVIEW

Question	**Answer**
1. What ocean is on the West coast of the U.S.?	• Pacific Ocean
2. What ocean is on the east coast of the U. S.?	• Atlantic Ocean
3. Name <u>one</u> of the two longest rivers in the U.S.	• Mississippi River • Missouri River

4. Name <u>one</u> state that borders Canada.

• Maine	• New Hampshire
• Vermont	• New York
• Ohio	• Pennsylvania
• Michigan	• North Dakota
• Minnesota	• Montana
• Idaho	• Washington
• Alaska	

5. Name <u>one</u> state that borders Mexico.

• California	• Arizona
• Texas	• New Mexico

6. Name <u>one</u> U.S. territory.

• Puerto Rico	• the Virgin Islands
• Guam	• American Samoa

7. Name <u>one</u> American Indian tribe in the U.S.

• Navajo	• Hopi
• Apache	• Chippewa
• Huron	• Seminole
• Pueblo	• Iroquois

LESSON 26

THE UNITED STATES GROWS
(2000 AND BEYOND)

OBJECTIVE

• Identify major events during the 2000s

PRE–READING

Oral

Look at the picture. Do you know what happened on September 11, 2001?

INFORMATION: September 11, 2001

Events	Results
Four airplanes were hijacked **by terrorists**	Nearly 3000 people died
Three planes crashed into public buildings	The World Trade Center (Twin Towers) in New York was destroyed
One plane crashed on the ground	The Pentagon in Washington, D.C., was damaged
First time U.S. was ever attacked	**Department of Homeland Security** was formed

Using the Information

A. Discuss this information with a partner.

    1. Why do you think this happened?

    2. What do you think the terrorists were trying to do or say?

    3. What is your reaction to this event?

READING: The Growth Continues

The United States is still growing. There are now over 300,000,000 people in the U.S. Other countries in the world are growing, too. China and India are demanding more oil. Prices of gasoline are going up in the U.S. and around the world.

Using the Reading

B. Look at the timeline below. Try to predict what will happen.

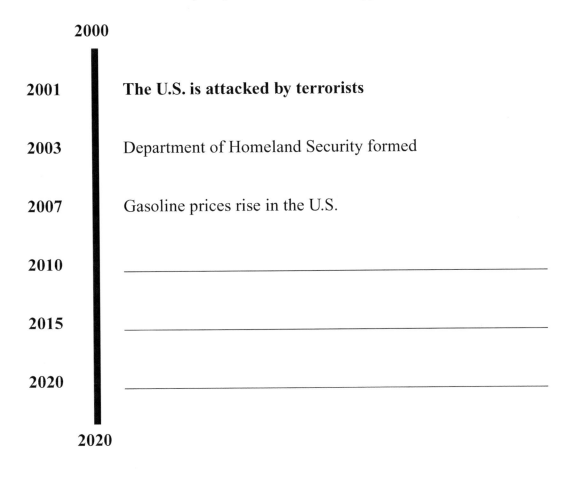

2000

2001   **The U.S. is attacked by terrorists**

2003   Department of Homeland Security formed

2007   Gasoline prices rise in the U.S.

2010   _____

2015   _____

2020   _____

2020

REVIEW

Question	Answer
1. What major event happened on September 11, 2001?	• terrorists attacked the U.S.

NATIONAL SYMBOLS

OBJECTIVE

- Identify ten national symbols

PRE–READING

Oral

Look at the pictures below. Write the names below under the pictures you know.

White House   **U.S. Capitol**   **Liberty Bell**   **Lincoln Memorial**

1. _____

2. _____

3. _____

4. _____

Vocabulary

Read the following words and definitions.

exhibit—a collection of objects usually found in a museum; the objects can be letters, things from a house, clothing, musical instruments, photographs, paintings, etc. People look at exhibits in museums to find information about a subject like the Civil War or the history of immigration in the U.S.

inauguration—the ceremony when the president takes office
The 20th Amendment says each inauguration for president must be on January 20th.

memorial—a building or statue to remember a famous person or time in history
The Vietnam Memorial in Washington, D.C., is a long black wall with a list of names of people who died during the Vietnam War.

monument—like a memorial; a building to remember someone or something important
Many tourists like to visit the national monuments in the U.S.

pledge—a promise; like an oath
Many children say the Pledge of Allegiance to the U.S. flag in school.

statue—an object made to look like or represent a person; usually made of stone, wood, or metal
One park in Washington, D.C., has a statue of George Washington sitting on a horse.

symbol—something that represents something else
The flag is often a symbol for a country. "$" is a symbol for U.S. money.

INFORMATION 1: Four National Symbols of the U.S.

THE AMERICAN FLAG

- 13 stripes: 7 red and 6 white for the first 13 states

- 50 stars (one for each state)

- Represents freedom and justice

THE STATUE OF LIBERTY

- Symbol for immigrants—many immigrants saw this statue when they arrived by boat

- Represents freedom, opportunity, and international friendship

- In New York City

INDEPENDENCE HALL

- Meeting place for the Continental Congresses before the War for Independence and for the first government of the U.S.

- Declaration of Independence and U.S. Constitution written and signed here

- In Philadelphia

LIBERTY BELL

- Symbol of freedom

- Rang on July 4, 1776, for our national holiday, Independence Day

- Has a famous crack

- In Liberty Bell Center (Philadelphia)

For the People

Using the Information

A. Write the answers to the following questions.

1. Which national symbol is found in New York City?

_____

_____

2. What do the stripes on the U.S. flag represent?

_____

_____

3. Where was the Declaration of Independence signed?

_____

_____

READING 1: The American Flag and the Statue of Liberty

Many people around the world know the American Flag. It has three names: *Old Glory*, *Stars and Stripes*, and the *Star–Spangled Banner*. The third name is also the name of our national song.

The flag represents freedom and justice in the U.S. It has three colors: red, white, and blue. **There are 13 red and white stripes. These stripes represent the original 13 states in the United States of America.** There is a field of blue with white stars. In 2008, there were 50 stars. **Each star represents one of the states in the U.S.**

People put up flags on special holidays. Government office buildings put up a flag every morning and take it down every evening. There are special ways to take care of the U.S. flag.

Students say the Pledge of Allegiance to the flag in many schools. This is the pledge: I pledge allegiance to the flag of the United States of America and to the Republic for which it stands, one nation, under God, indivisible, with liberty and justice for all. **This pledge says you are loyal to the U.S., and the states are united as one nation with liberty and justice for everyone.** Sometimes they also sing the *Star–Spangled Banner*. This song, written during the War of 1812, is **America's national anthem**.

The **Statue of Liberty** was a gift from France in 1886. It represents freedom, opportunity for Americans, and international friendship. In the early 1900s, many immigrants came by boat to the U.S. They saw the statue on **Liberty Island in New York City harbor**. It was their first sight of America.

There is a museum in the bottom part of the statue. It has exhibits about the history of immigration in the U.S. There are many pictures, letters, and objects from the native countries of the immigrants.

Using the Reading

B. Bring a picture or drawing of your country's flag to class. Tell the class about your flag. These are some questions to think about:

What do the colors of the flag represent?

If there is a picture on the flag, what does it represent?

Are there special times when people put up flags in your country?

C. Listen to your teacher read the Pledge of Allegiance aloud. Practice reading it aloud with a partner.

INFORMATION 2: Six National Symbols in Washington, D.C.

THE U.S. CAPITOL

- Meeting place for the U.S. Congress: Senate and House of Representatives

- Place for the inauguration of most presidents

THE WHITE HOUSE

- Official home for presidents (except George Washington)

- Address: 1600 Pennsylvania Avenue

- Burned during War of 1812 and rebuilt after the war

WASHINGTON MONUMENT

- Built to remember George Washington, the first president

- 555 feet high

- Visitors may go up to the top of the building

LINCOLN MEMORIAL

- Built to remember Abraham Lincoln, the 16th president

- Has a very large statue of Lincoln sitting in it

- Has two famous speeches by Lincoln on the walls

JEFFERSON MEMORIAL

- Built to remember Thomas Jefferson, the third president

- Has a large statue of Jefferson standing

NATIONAL ARCHIVES

- Has exhibits with the original Declaration of Independence, the U.S. Constitution, and the Bill of Rights

- It keeps and protects other important documents

Using the Information

D. Read the following sentences. Do you think they are true (T) or false (F)? Circle **T** or **F**.

1. The president lives at the U.S. Capitol.   T   F

2. The U.S. Capitol is in Washington, D.C.   T   F

3. The Declaration of Independence was signed at the National Archives.   T   F

4. The Washington Monument is a statue of George Washington.   T   F

5. Some memorials in Washington, D.C., honor U.S. presidents.   T   F

6. You can find some of Abraham Lincoln's speeches on the walls of his memorial.   T   F

READING 2: The U.S. Capitol and the White House

Two important buildings in **Washington, D.C.**, are national symbols. The U.S. Capitol is a symbol for our legislative branch of government. The senators and the representatives meet at the Capitol. They make the laws for the U.S. Every four years, on January 20th, we have an inauguration ceremony for the president. Most inaugurations are in the Capitol.

The **White House** is the symbol for the executive branch of our government. It is the **home and office** for the president. The president often meets his advisors, members of Congress, and representatives from foreign governments at the White House. Special dinners and events take place at the White House.

Using the Reading

E. Work with a small group. Complete the following chart. Think about three different countries.

Country	Home for the Leader	Place for Making Laws	Name of One National Symbol

REVIEW

Question	Answer
1. What do we show loyalty to when we say the Pledge of Allegiance?	• the United States • the flag
2. Why does the flag have 13 stripes?	• because there were 13 original colonies • to represent the original colonies
3. Why does the flag have 50 stars?	• because there is one star for each state • because each star represents a state • because there are 50 states
4. What is the name of the national anthem?	• the Star–Spangled Banner
5. Where is the Statue of Liberty?	• New York City harbor • Liberty Island
6. What is the capital of the United States?	• Washington, D.C.

THE UNITED STATES AND CITIZENSHIP

OBJECTIVE

• Identify specific duties and rights of citizens

PRE-READING

Oral

Look at the pictures below. They show some of the responsibilities of U.S. citizens.

Discuss the following questions with the class.

1. What are five responsibilities you see in the pictures?

2. Which responsibilities are the same in your country?

3. What other responsibilities do you have in your country?

4. Are there other responsibilities for U.S. citizens?

Vocabulary

Match the words on the left with the definitions on the right. Put the correct letter on the line. You can use a dictionary for help.

_____ 1. **duty**   a) to follow laws or rules

_____ 2. (to) **register**   b) safety; taking care of someone or something

_____ 3. (to) **obey**   c) something you have to do; responsibility

_____ 4. **protection**   d) to put your name on a list

INFORMATION: Duties of U.S. Citizens and Why They Are Important

Duties	Why?
Obey Laws	Laws protect the people. A basic right for all people is protection.
Vote	The U.S. is a representative democracy. All citizens have to vote to choose good people to be representatives.
Pay taxes	The government needs money to pay for services (for example, police and military protection). **Taxes must be paid by April 15th**.
Be on a jury when called	Everyone has the right to a trial with a jury (6th Amendment). Members of a jury must be U.S. citizens.
Register with the military	If there is a war, the military may need more soldiers. **All <u>men</u> between the ages of 18 and 26 must register with the Selective Service.**

Using the Information

A. The chart tells you about the duties of U.S. citizens. It also tells you the reason these duties are important.

1. What is the title of this chart?

_____

2. How many duties do you see? _____

3. What is the heading of the second column? _____

4. Why do citizens have to vote? _____

_____

5. Why do citizens have to be part of a jury? _____

READING 1: Rights of U.S. Citizens

Who is a U.S. citizen? A person born in the U.S. is a citizen. If a U.S. citizen has a baby in another country, the baby may be a U.S. citizen. Resident aliens can become citizens after they live legally in the U.S. for at least 5 years and take a citizenship exam. If they pass the exam, they can become naturalized citizens.

Both U.S.–born and naturalized citizens have many extra rights. **Only citizens can vote in U.S. elections. They can work for the federal government. They can travel with U.S. passports. They can apply to bring their family to the U.S. Only citizens can be members of a jury.** Naturalized citizens do not have one special right. Naturalized citizens cannot become president or vice president of the U.S. But, a naturalized citizen can be a senator, representative, governor, mayor, etc.

Using the Reading

B. Unscramble the following sentences. Look at the Reading to help you. The first word of each sentence has a capital letter.

1. citizens / some / are / for / There / only / rights /

_____

_____

2. is / in / born / a / A / U.S. / the / person / citizen /

_____

_____

3. vote / citizens / Only / can / elections / in /

_____

_____

4. U.S. / travel / with / They / passport / can / a /

_____

_____

5. president / U.S. / citizens / Naturalized / cannot / of / vice president / become / the / or /

_____

_____

C. Form a small group. Discuss the following questions with your group. Then share your group's answers with the class.

When do people pay taxes in the U.S.?

What kind of taxes do people pay in the U.S.?

What does the government do with our tax money?

Do you think U.S. taxes are higher or lower than taxes in other countries?

READING 2: Being a Good Citizen

When you become a citizen, you make promises. **You say you will give up your loyalty to other countries. You say you will defend the Constitution and laws of the United States. You say you will obey the laws of the U.S.** You must swear to this Oath of Allegiance.

Being a good citizen means **participating in democracy**. It means that you should **vote** in elections. You should **join a political party**. We have two major political parties in the U.S.: the **Republicans and the Democrats. (The current president is a Democrat.)** You should also **join community or civic groups**. You should read about what is happening in the local newspaper, and sometimes **write to the newspaper**. All these things will make you a better citizen.

Using the Reading

D. Discuss the following with a partner.

1. Why you should vote

2. Why you should join a community group

3. Why you should read the newspaper

REVIEW

Question	Answer
1. What is <u>one</u> responsibility that is only for United States citizens?	• to vote • to serve on a jury
2. What are <u>two</u> rights that are only for U.S. citizens?	• to vote • to work for the federal government • to carry a U.S. passport • to serve on a jury
3. When is the last day you can send in federal income tax forms?	• April 15
4. When must all men register for the Selective Service?	• at age 18 • between 18 and 26 years
5. What is <u>one</u> promise you make when you become a U.S. citizen?	• to give up loyalty to other countries • to defend the Constitution and laws of the United States • to obey the law
6. What are <u>two</u> ways that Americans can participate in their democracy?	• to vote • to join a political party • to write to a newspaper • to join a civic or community group
7. What are the two major political parties in the U.S.?	• Republican and Democratic
8. What is the political party of the president now?	• Democratic (2009)

LESSON 29

THE U.S. AND CITIZENSHIP—
THE REQUIREMENTS FOR NATURALIZATION

OBJECTIVE

- Identify the process for naturalization

PRE-READING

Oral

Form a small group. Read the list below. These are some reasons people want to become U.S. citizens. Can you think of two other reasons? Write them below.

1. They want to vote.

2. They want to bring some other members of their family to the U.S.

3. They want to help their communities.

4. _____

5. _____

Some people cannot become U.S. citizens. Here are two reasons. Can you think of more reasons? Write them below.

1. The person has lived in the U.S. for only two years.

2. The person broke some laws in the U.S. and went to jail for one year.

3. _____

4. _____

5. _____

Vocabulary

Read the following words and definitions.

(to) deport—to make someone who is not a citizen leave a country

dictator—the head of a country; this person has all the power and makes all the laws

(to) gamble—to take chances with money; to make or lose money by playing cards, games, horses, etc.

oath of allegiance—a serious promise to be loyal

good moral character—the qualities of a person who behaves in a lawful and correct way, according to the rules of society

Written

Read the following situations about permanent residents. Do you think the person can apply for citizenship? Check (✔) **Yes** or **No**.

	YES	NO
1. Juanita came to the U.S. 2 years ago.	____	____
2. Sam is a good worker and is studying English and about the U.S. government.	____	____
3. Makiesse is 17 years old. She came to the U.S. 6 years ago.	____	____

INFORMATION: The Requirements for Naturalization

There are many requirements to become a U.S. citizen. These are the most important ones:

You must:
- **be 18+ years old.**
- **be a permanent resident for 5 years or more.**
- **be loyal to the U.S.**
- **be able to read, write, speak, and understand basic English.**
- **have good moral character.**
- **understand the U.S. government structure and the Constitution.**
- **take an oath of allegiance to the U.S.**

Using the Information

A. Complete the following exercise. Look at the Information above to find the words to write in the blanks.

If you want to apply for **1)** _____, you must

be 18 **2)** _____ old or more. You must be a permanent

3) _____ for 5 years or more. This means you have lived

legally in the U.S. for at least **4)** _____ years.

You must know some **5)** _____ so you can read, speak,

and write it. You must also know about the U.S. **6)** _____

and about the U.S. Constitution. It is important to be loyal to your new country

and to take an **7)** _____ of allegiance. Another requirement

is to have good moral **8)** _____. This means you

are not a bad person.

READING: Requirements to Apply for Naturalization

Immigrants must meet certain requirements when they apply for naturalization. For example, they must be at least 18 years old and be legal residents of the U.S. for at least 5 years. They apply for naturalization in the state where they live. They must live in that state for the last 6 months (or more) of those 5 years. They do not have to live in the U.S. every day for 5 years, but they cannot live outside the U.S. for:

    a) a period of 1 year or more, or

    b) a total of 30 months or more.

Many immigrants ask about the requirement for good moral character. The USCIS explains that to become a U.S. citizen a person cannot be someone who:

    a) drinks too much;

    b) is married to two or more people at the same time;

    c) sells his or her body for sexual pleasure;

    d) buys, sells, or uses drugs;

    e) gambles illegally;

    f) is a criminal;

    g) was convicted of a crime in the U.S. and was in jail for 6+ months;

    h) was convicted of killing another person without a legal reason;

    i) was a member of a Communist Party during the 10 years before applying for naturalization (except if forced to join, or under 16 years old);

    j) wants a dictator to rule the U.S., or wants to use violence against the U.S. government or government officers; or,

    k) the government is trying to deport.

The USCIS also thinks about the age of the people applying for naturalization. If someone is 50 years old and has lived in the U.S. for 20+ years as a permanent resident, that person does not have to meet the English language requirement.

There are four steps to naturalization.

Step 1: <u>The Application</u>: You must completely fill out the application which is **N–400**. You must send that application, a check for $675 and two passport–size photographs to the right USCIS office.

Step 2: <u>Fingerprinting</u>. You will receive a letter from the USCIS office to go for fingerprinting.

Step 3: <u>The Interview</u>. After you are fingerprinted, you will be asked to go to a USCIS interview. You will be asked questions about U.S. history and U.S. government. You have practiced those questions already. You will also be asked to demonstrate your basic knowledge of oral and written English.

Step 4: <u>Notification</u>. After the interview, you will either receive an invitation to a "swearing–in" ceremony, or a letter telling you why your citizenship was denied. If you failed the English or history and government exams, the USCIS officer will give you a new date to retake the exams.

Using the Reading

B. Read the situations about permanent residents again. Use the Information and the Reading. Can the person apply for citizenship? Check (✔) **Yes** or **No**.

	<u>YES</u>	<u>NO</u>
1. Juanita came to the U.S. 2 years ago.	____	____
2. Sam is a good worker and is studying English and about the U.S. government. He has worked in Michigan for 7 years.	____	____
3. Omar sent his N–400 and two pictures to USCIS.	____	____
4. Makiesse is 17 years old. She came to the U.S. 6 years ago.	____	____
5. Henri is married to Caroline. Caroline is a U.S. citizen. Henri has lived in the U.S. for 4 years.	____	____
6. Jan does not work. Jan steals things from stores and sells them. Jan went to jail for 10 months last year.	____	____
7. Ferdosi came to the U.S. when she was 14. Now she is 20. She goes to college and works part–time at a hospital. Her friends say she is a good person.	____	____
8. Estella became a permanent resident 7 years ago. She lived in California for many years. Three months ago she moved to Virginia. She works as a computer programmer. She does not gamble or use drugs.	____	____

YES   NO

9. Karol is from Bulgaria. He became a permanent resident
5 years ago. He works with his brother as a house painter.
Karol never learned English. He speaks only Bulgarian
with his brother.

      ____   ____

C. Work with a partner. Think about five friends who are immigrants living in the U.S.
Does each friend meet all these requirements? Write their names in the box below. Put a
check (✔) under the requirements they meet.

NAME	AGE	PERMANENT RESIDENT	YEARS OF RESIDENCE	GOOD CHARACTER	KNOWS ENGLISH	KNOWS GOVERNMENT
1.						
2.						
3.						
4.						
5.						

REVIEW

Question

1. Name <u>five</u> of the important
requirements for naturalization.

Answer

• be 18+ years old
• be a permanent resident for 5 years
  or more
• be loyal to the U.S.
• be able to read, write, speak, and
  understand basic English
• have good moral character
• understand the U.S. government
  structure and the Constitution
• take an oath of allegiance to the U.S.

GENERAL REVIEW—
U.S. GOVERNMENT

THE CONSTITUTION

If you need help with these exercises, you can look back at the lessons.

A. Complete the following crossword puzzle.

ACROSS

3 The first ten amendments (three words)

5 Congress is in the _____ branch.

9 Senate + House of Representatives =

12 The president is head of the _____ branch.

13 The First Amendment guarantees _____ of press and religion.

15 An addition to the U.S. Constitution

DOWN

1 Symbol for the U.S. It is red, white, and blue.

2 There are two _____; the White _____ and the _____ of Representatives.

4 If you go to court, a _____ can help you.

6 We _____ a president every 4 years.

7 Separation of _____

8 The 19th Amendment says women can _____.

10 The 1st Amendment gives us freedom of _____. We can say our thoughts.

11 To take back; the 21st Amendment _____ed the 18th Amendment.

14 How many U.S. Supreme Courts are in the U.S. government?

B. Read the following groups of sentences. One sentence is false in each group. Circle the letter of the false one.

1. a) We have four levels of government in the U.S.: international, federal, state, and local.

   b) The Constitution is for all people in the U.S.

   c) We have a democracy in the U.S.

2. a) The U.S. Constitution is over 300 years old.

   b) Separation of powers is one of the three main principles of the Constitution.

   c) A constitution gives a plan to rule a country.

3. a) The Preamble is an introduction to the Constitution.

   b) The writers of the Constitution wanted peace in the country.

   c) The Constitution says the U.S. cannot fight in a war.

4. a) There are three branches in the U.S. government.

   b) Article I says the executive makes the laws.

   c) Article V discusses the amendment process.

5. a) The Bill of Rights is the first five amendments of the Constitution.

   b) The Bill of Rights gives us freedom of speech and religion.

   c) The Bill of Rights gives us the right to a trial.

6. a) In 1987, the Constitution had 26 amendments.

   b) The amendments give black people, women, and people over 16 years old the right to vote.

   c) Some amendments discuss elections.

C. Now write those six false sentences. Make them true.

1. _____

   _____

2. _____

   _____

3. _____

   _____

4. _____

   _____

5. _____

   _____

6. _____

   _____

D. Match the information on the left with its location in the Constitution. Put the correct letter on the line.

_____ 1. We have the right to a lawyer.

_____ 2. Congress passes laws.

_____ 3. Three–fourths of the states must approve an amendment.

_____ 4. We can elect a president for only two terms.

_____ 5. We have the right to say our thoughts.

_____ 6. The president is the commander in chief of the army and navy.

_____ 7. The judicial branch decides if laws are okay.

_____ 8. We want liberty for ourselves and our children.

a) Preamble

b) Article I

c) Article II

d) Article III

e) Article V

f) Amendment 1

g) Amendment 6

h) Amendment 22

E. Look at these pictures again. What does the Constitution tell us about them? Share your ideas with the class.

THE FEDERAL GOVERNMENT

Three Branches of the Federal Government

A. Complete the following crossword puzzle.

ACROSS

   3 The federal government has ___ branches.

   6 The executive branch enforces the ___ .

   9 No branch has more ___ than the other branches.

   10 The head of the executive branch is the ___ .

   11 The Congress ___ the laws.

DOWN

   1 Each branch has its own ___ .

   2 The branches have ___ powers.

   4 One part of Congress is the ___ of Representatives.

   5 The highest court in the U.S. is the ___ Court.

   7 The U.S. government has a system of ___ and balances.

   8 The second part of the Congress is the ___ . (see 4, Down)

Federal Officials

B. Work with a partner. One student will look at the first chart. The other student will look at the second chart. You can see that your chart is not complete. Do not look at your partner's chart. You can ask your partner questions to get the information you need. For example, you can ask, "How old does the vice president have to be?" Complete the chart:

	President	Vice President	Senator	Representative
Age	35+ years		30+ years	
Citizen		born in U.S.		7+ years
Residence		14+ years		in state
Term	4 years		6 years	
Limit	2 terms		none	
Number of:	1			435

	President	Vice President	Senator	Representative
Age		35+ years		25+ years
Citizen	born in U.S.		9+ years	
Residence	14+ years		in state	
Term		4 years		2 years
Limit		2 terms		none
Number of:		1	100	

Candidates

C. Read the short descriptions of these candidates. Can they be candidates for President (Pres.), Vice President (V.P.), Senator (Sen.) or Representative (Rep.)? Look at the chart you completed on page 162. Put a check (✔) next to <u>all</u> of the offices they can be candidates for.

	Pres.	**V.P.**	**Sen.**	**Rep.**
1. Amelia Soares, 40. Born in Brazil. U.S. citizen and living in Texas since 1960.	_____	_____	✔	✔
2. Rose Moradian, 60. Born in Hawaii. Living in Hawaii all her life.	_____	_____	_____	_____
3. James Carter, 84. Born in Georgia. Was U.S. President from 1977–1981.	_____	_____	_____	_____
4. William Clinton, 62. Born in Arkansas. Was U.S. President from 1993–2001.	_____	_____	_____	_____
5. Thomas Fondell, 29. Born in Minnesota. Living in Africa since 1980.	_____	_____	_____	_____
6. Elisabeth Bailey, 58. Born in Vermont. Living in Vermont since 1980.	_____	_____	_____	_____
7. Christine Purdy, 32. Born in Missouri. Living in Washington for 6 years.	_____	_____	_____	_____

Check your answers. Did the other students check the same offices?

Federal Checks and Balances

D. The three branches of government are represented by the buildings below. Fill in the name of each branch.

_____   _____   _____

     BRANCH   BRANCH   BRANCH

List three duties for each branch.

1._____   4._____   7._____

2._____   5._____   8._____

3._____   6._____   9._____

Write one way each branch checks the other two branches.

CHECKS EXECUTIVE: CHECKS LEGISLATIVE: CHECKS LEGISLATIVE:

1. _____   3. _____   5. _____

CHECKS JUDICIAL: CHECKS JUDICIAL: CHECKS EXECUTIVE:

2. _____   4. _____   6. _____

Our Leaders Today

E. Find the names of some important leaders in the U.S. You can ask your family, friends, or teacher. You can hear about them on TV or read about them in the newspaper.

U.S. President _____

Vice President _____

Your Senators to Congress _____

_____

Your Representative to Congress _____

The Cabinet

F. The Cabinet members advise the President. Can you find the names of the different Cabinet offices that are listed? Circle these words in the puzzle.

State
Labor
Homeland
Health
Energy
Housing
Justice
Interior
Defense
Commerce
Treasury
Education
Agriculture
Transportation

```
I X O W J F Y D T Z O H P O B
W L J V H I Y E R P I Q R F D
C O M M E R C E A Z X H R Y Q
S T R Z A N S P N C S O A R E
A R H S L I J P S Q U M G I N
Q E D K T R J R P L Y E R I E
K A E W H O W N O U F L I B R
A S F L A B O R R Z E A C L G
X U E E D U C A T I O N U J Y
W R N H O Z D J A Z H D L U E
Q Y S T A T E V T T X T T S Z
A O E I N T E R I O R R U T J
B E X R J Q F N O R T I R I K
M H P H O U S I N G D J E C K
B C U X Z Q F W V R F C B E W
```

Judicial Branch

G. The federal court system has District Courts, Circuit Courts of Appeals, and a Supreme Court. Fill in the correct information:

First, a federal case starts in a _____ court.

Second, the case can be reviewed in an _____ court.

Third, if necessary, a final review can be made in the _____ Court.

H. You are a Supreme Court Justice. Read the laws below. Are these laws constitutional? You must vote on each law. Write "Yes" if the law is constitutional. Write "No" if the law is unconstitutional.

VOTE

1. Today's president will become president for life. _____

2. All states will have the same number of senators. _____

3. The state of California can say "NO" to all new immigrants. _____

4. The people will vote for Supreme Court justices. _____

5. Every state will print money for that state. _____

6. All citizens can have a lawyer. _____

7. You must be a citizen for 10 years before you can vote. _____

8. All children must pray in public schools. _____

9. Newspapers can make jokes about the president. _____

GENERAL GOVERNMENT REVIEW

Leaders

A. We have different names for many leaders in our three levels of government. There is a list of those names below. Can you find the names in the word search? Circle the words.

~~President~~
Governor
Representative
Senator
Assemblyman
Mayor
City Council
Supervisor
Justice
Officials

```
M  A  Y  S  S  R  Z  J  U  S  T  I  C  E  E
O  F  N  E  U  B  R  E  P  R  E  S  I  U  V
F  V  Z  N (P  R  E  S  I  D  E  N  T) U  S
F  G  O  A  E  V  U  B  J  Z  M  A  Y  O  R
I  E  N  T  R  M  H  J  X  Y  P  R  C  D  N
C  A  G  O  V  E  R  N  O  R  R  I  O  U  N
I  X  G  R  I  M  A  X  I  C  E  A  U  L  X
A  N  A  S  S  E  M  B  L  Y  M  A  N  I  S
L  A  X  D  O  K  C  C  E  A  Y  X  C  Z  P
S  R  E  P  R  E  S  E  N  T  A  T  I  V  E
P  E  S  A  R  D  B  O  U  C  I  L  L  E  V
```

Petitions

B. Form a small group. Choose one topic.

1. You want to change a law in your state.

2. You want to write a new law.

3. You want the state or local government to give money to build a hospital or school or more roads.

Discuss your choice. If you want one of these things to happen, what can you do? Write a group petition. Say what you want. Give your reasons. Give ideas to make this happen. Share your petition with the class. Do your classmates agree with your ideas? Have a class vote on each petition.

Responsibilities of Government

C. Look at the following list. These are responsibilities or actions of the different levels of government. List them in the correct column in the chart below.

passes state laws	gives money for defense
collects federal taxes	School Board of Education
water department	National Guard
driver's licenses	cases between citizens of two states
parking ticket	cases between citizens of same state
makes treaties	rules for trade in one state
prints money	rules for international trade
city council	fire department

Federal	State	Local

For the People

Important Documents

D. Read the following phrases. They can be found in different official documents. Match the phrase on the left with its document on the right. Put the correct letter on the line.

_____ 1. "We the people of the United States…"

a) Articles of the Constitution

_____ 2. "The citizens will elect a governor every 4 years…"

b) Bill of Rights

_____ 3. "The mayor and city council will be the executive and legislative branches…"

c) Amendments 11–26

_____ 4. "…freedom of religion, speech, press…"

d) Preamble

_____ 5. "…citizens 18 years or older can vote…"

e) a state constitution

_____ 6. "As of May 12, 2008, first class letters need a 42¢ stamp."

f) a state law

_____ 7. "Everyone must pass a driving test to get a license."

g) a local charter

_____ 8. "Three–fourths (3/4) of the states must vote to amend the Constitution."

h) a federal law

Number Game

E. You need to remember some important numbers in the U.S. government. Fill in the blanks below with the correct numbers:

1. branches in the U.S. government   _____

2. senators in the U.S. Congress   _____

3. representatives in the U.S. Congress   _____

4. vice president(s) in the executive branch   _____

5. Supreme Court justices   _____

6. states   _____

7. amendments in the Bill of Rights   _____

8. George Washington was president # _____.   _____

9. In 2008, the U.S. Constitution was _____ years old _____

Now add these numbers   = _____

Your answer has three numbers. Each number represents a letter. Use the chart below. Find the numbers from your answer and their letters.

0	1	2	3	4	5	6	7	8	9
A	E	P	S	O	T	L	R	U	D

Write the letters in the same order. You will see the name of a special place for you.

_____ _____ _____

For the People

LESSON 31

GENERAL REVIEW—
U.S. HISTORY

EARLY AMERICA

If you need help with these exercises you can look back at the lessons.

The Early Years of America

A. Read the following descriptions of people, documents, and holidays. Choose one of the terms from the box below to answer the questions.

~~Bill of Rights~~   **Articles of Confederation**   **U.S. Constitution**

George Washington   **Thomas Jefferson**   **Independence Day**

Presidents' Day   **Thanksgiving**   **Declaration of Independence**

1. This document guarantees certain rights and liberties for Americans. What is it?

   Bill of Rights

2. I wrote most of the Declaration of Independence. Who am I?

3. We celebrate this holiday on the 4th of July. What is it?

4. This document explained the rules for the first U.S. government. It was not very good because the central government was weak. What is it?

5. This holiday was the first American holiday. We celebrate it in November. What is it?

6. This document said the American colonies wanted to be free. What is it?

7. This holiday honors George Washington and Abraham Lincoln. We celebrate it in February. What is it?

_____

8. This document explains the U.S. system of government. It tells about three branches: executive, legislative, and judicial. What is it?

_____

9. I was the first U.S. president. Who am I?

_____

B. Complete the timeline below. It tells about some important events in early America. Fill in the correct dates and actions.

1492   _____ sailed to _____

_____   Jamestown Colony began.

1620   _____

1775–1783   _____

_____   Representatives signed the Declaration of Independence.

1787   _____

_____   George Washington became the first president.

C. Locate the following places on the map below. Write the name next to the letter.

Georgia   **Massachusetts**   **New York**

Jamestown   **Philadelphia**

B. _____

A. _____

Boston

New York City

Pennsylvania

C. _____

Virginia

D. _____

E. _____

The 1800s

A. Read the following words of different people from the 1800s. Whom do you think said these words? Choose a person from the box below. Write the names on the lines.

Abraham Lincoln	**an abolitionist**
a factory worker	**a factory owner**
a plantation owner	**an ex–slave**

1. "I hate working long hours in this hot place with noisy machines."

   _____

2. "We need tariffs to help American industry grow."

   _____

3. "Because of the 13th, 14th, and 15th Amendments, I am a free man. I am a citizen and I can vote."

   _____

4. "We need slaves to plant and pick our cotton."

   _____

5. "This country will not divide…a government of the people, by the people, for the people shall not perish from this earth."

   _____

6. "Slavery takes away individual freedoms. We must fight the South to put an end to slavery."

   _____

B. The U.S. flag has many names:

STARS AND STRIPES

OLD GLORY

THE _____ _____ _____

C. Form a small group. The timeline below has a little information about the 1800s. Discuss other important events of the 1800s (examples: wars, inventions, speeches, elections, etc.). Add five to seven more events to the timeline. Put the specific date on the right side of the timeline. Write the events next to the dates. Share your group's timeline with the class.

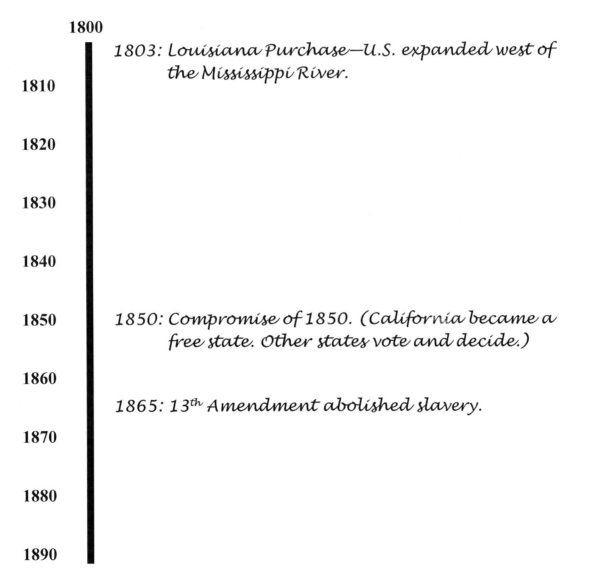

1800

1803: Louisiana Purchase—U.S. expanded west of the Mississippi River.

1810

1820

1830

1840

1850

1850: Compromise of 1850. (California became a free state. Other states vote and decide.)

1860

1865: 13th Amendment abolished slavery.

1870

1880

1890

D. Work with a partner. One person looks at Outline 1 below. The other person looks at Outline 2 on page 177. Take turns asking questions to get the information you need to complete your outline. Write the new information on the lines.

Outline 1

I. Wars in the 1800s

    A. War of 1812 (1812–1814)

    B. _____

    C. Civil War (1861–1865)

II. Reasons Americans wanted to go west

    A. _____

    B. to get more good farmland

    C. _____

    D. to find gold

III. Differences between the North and the South

    A. _____

    B. tariffs

    C. _____

Outline 2

I. Wars in the 1800s

    A. _____

    B. Mexican–American War (1846–1848)

    C. _____

II. Reasons Americans wanted to go west

    A. to transport goods on the Mississippi River

    B. _____

    C. to get land for raising cattle

    D. _____

III. Differences between the North and the South

    A. ways to make money

    B. _____

    C. representation in Congress

E. The chart below shows you some of the important differences between the North and the South that caused the Civil War. Complete the chart.

Differences	NORTH	SOUTH
Ways to make money		
Tariffs		
Representation		
Ideas about the Federal Government		

F. Use the map and key to fill in the blanks.

1. Name three states with a lot of farms.

_____ _____ _____

2. Name three states with cotton plantations.

_____ _____ _____

3. Name three states with a lot of cattle.

_____ _____ _____

4. Name three states with a lot of factories.

_____ _____ _____

5. Name two states with gold.

_____ _____

6. Name two states with steel industries.

_____   _____

U.S. History (1600–2008)

A. The U.S. has fought in many wars. Complete the names of the wars below. Each space (__) equals one letter. The dates on the left will help you remember the names.

1. 1763   The French and __ __ __ __ __ __ War

2. 1775–1783   The __ __ __ __ __ __ __ __ __ __ __ __ __ War

            or the War for __ __ __ __ __ __ __ __ __ __ __ __

3. 1812–1814   The War __ __ 1812

4. 1861–1865   The __ __ __ __ __ War

5. 1914–1918   __ __ __ __ __ War I

6. 1941–1944   World __ __ __ II

7. 1950–1953   The __ __ __ __ __ __ War

8. 1960–1973   The __ __ __ __ __ __ __ War

9. 1990–1991   The __ __ __ __ War

10. 2003–   The War in __ __ __ __

Circle the words from the wars in the puzzle below.

```
B  T  C  I  V  I  L  I  V  D  I  P  F  R  S
Y  R  E  V  O  L  U  T  I  O  N  A  R  Y  G
K  H  Y  L  U  F  D  D  E  B  D  Q  Z  J  U
O  O  F  V  L  I  K  P  T  Y  I  X  A  U  L
R  A  J  N  T  H  G  F  N  H  A  O  O  F  F
E  S  W  O  R  L  D  V  A  H  N  Q  H  H  A
A  T  A  L  I  R  A  Q  M  T  Z  S  E  T  F
N  R  R  I  N  D  E  P  E  N  D  E  N  C  E
```

B. We remember many important times in history on holidays. When are these holidays? Write the month on the line after the holiday.

January   **February**   **July**   **November**

1. Thanksgiving _____

2. Independence Day _____

3. Martin Luther King, Jr., Day _____

4. Veterans Day _____

5. Presidents' Day _____

Do you know why these holidays are important?

_____

_____

C. Read the paragraphs below. Then complete the following outline.

The Expansion of the United States

The U.S. grew from two small colonies to a very large country. It began with the Jamestown and Plymouth colonies. They were on the east coast of North America in the early 1600s. More people came to settle until Colonial America had 13 colonies. At first, the 13 colonies were part of England. Then, the men fought a war for independence in 1776. After the Revolutionary War, the colonies became 13 states.

The United States of America did not stop growing. In the 1800s, settlers moved west, south, and north from the first 13 states. Many immigrants came to the U.S. in the 1800s. They needed land for their homes. They settled in the new territories.

The U.S. got more land in two ways:

1. The U.S. bought land, like the Louisiana Purchase; and
2. The U.S. got land from treaties after the U.S. Army won some wars. The U.S. got the territories of Texas, New Mexico, and Arizona from the Mexican–American War.

Also in the 1800s transportation helped the country grow larger. Men built railroads across the U.S. People could move more easily then. In the late 1800s, Henry Ford started producing cars. People used cars to travel.

During the 1900s, the U.S. did not get many new territories. The territories from the 1800s became states.

Outline

I. Colonial _____: pre–1800

    A. Jamestown and _____

    B. 13 _____

    C. War for _____

    D. _____ states

II. 1800s

    A. People moving west

        1. New settlers

        2. _____ from other countries

    B. New territories

        1. _____, like the Louisiana Purchase

        2. From war treaties, like _____

    C. Transportation

        1. _____

        2. _____

III. 1900s: Territories from the 1800s _____

D. You need to remember some important numbers and dates in U.S. history. Fill in the blanks on the right with the correct numbers or dates.

1. George Washington was the ___st president. _____

2. Abraham Lincoln was the ___th president. _____

3. The first colony at Jamestown began in ___. _____

4. There were ___ original colonies in 1783. _____

5. The Bill of Rights has ___ amendments. _____

6. They wrote the Declaration of Independence in ___. _____

7. We celebrate Independence Day on July ___th. _____

8. World War ___ was between 1914 and 1918. _____

9. Total number of amendments to the Constitution. _____

10. How many parts does Congress have? _____

Now add these numbers   = _____

Your answer has four numbers. Each number represents a letter. Use the chart below. Find the numbers from your answer and their letters.

1	2	3	4	5	6	7	8	9
U	S	V	O	T	R	E	D	Z

_____ _____ _____ _____

VOCABULARY INDEX

100 QUESTIONS FOR THE
NEW NATURALIZATION TEST

The 100 civics (history and government) questions and answers for the redesigned (new) naturalization test are listed below. Applicants who filed the Application for Naturalization, Form N–400, on or after October, 2008, should study this list. The civics test is an oral test and the USCIS Officer will ask the applicant up to 10 of the 100 civics questions. An applicant must answer 6 out of 10 questions correctly to pass the civics portion of the naturalization test.

* If you are 65 years old or older and have been a legal permanent resident of the United States for 20 or more years, you may study just the questions that have been marked with an asterisk.

AMERICAN GOVERNMENT

A. Principles of American Democracy

1. What is the supreme law of the land?
   • The Constitution

2. What does the Constitution do?
   • sets up the government
   • defines the government
   • protects basic rights of Americans

3. The idea of self–government is in the first three words of the Constitution. What are these words?
   • We the People

4. What is an amendment?
   • a change (to the Constitution)
   • an addition (to the Constitution)

5. What do we call the first ten amendments to the Constitution?
   • The Bill of Rights

6. What is <u>one</u> right or freedom in the First Amendment?*
   - speech
   - religion
   - assembly
   - press
   - petition the government

7. How many amendments does the Constitution have?
   - twenty–seven (27)

8. What did the Declaration of Independence do?
   - announced our independence (from Great Britain)
   - declared our independence (from Great Britain)
   - said that the United States is free (from Great Britain)

9. What are <u>two</u> rights in the Declaration of Independence?
   - life
   - liberty
   - pursuit of happiness

10. What is freedom of religion?
    - You can practice any religion, or not practice a religion.

11. What is the economic system in the United States?*
    - capitalist economy
    - market economy

12. What is the "rule of law"?
    - Everyone must follow the law.
    - Leaders must obey the law.
    - Government must obey the law.
    - No one is above the law.

B. System of Government

13. Name <u>one</u> branch or part of the government.*
    - Congress
    - legislative
    - president
    - executive
    - the courts
    - judicial

14. What stops one branch of government from becoming too powerful?
    • checks and balances
    • separation of powers

15. Who is in charge of the executive branch?
    • the President

16. Who makes federal laws?
    • Congress
    • Senate and House (of Representatives)
    • (U.S. or national) legislature

17. What are the two parts of the U.S. Congress?*
    • the Senate and House (of Representatives)

18. How many U.S. Senators are there?
    • one hundred (100)

19. We elect a U.S. Senator for how many years?
    • six (6)

20. Who is <u>one</u> of your state's U.S. Senators?*
    • Answers will vary.

21. The House of Representatives has how many voting members?
    • four hundred thirty–five (435)

22. We elect a U.S. Representative for how many years?
    • two (2)

23. Name your U.S. Representative.
    • Answers will vary.

24. Who does a U.S. Senator represent?
    • all people of the state

25. Why do some states have more Representatives than other states?
    • (because of) the state's population
    • (because) they have more people
    • (because) some states have more people

26. We elect a president for how many years?
   - four (4)

27. In what month do we vote for president?*
   - November

28. What is the name of the president of the United States now?*
   - Barack H. Obama
   - Barack Obama
   - Obama

29. What is the name of the Vice President of the United States now?
   - Joseph Biden
   - Joe Biden
   - Biden

30. If the president can no longer serve, who becomes president?
   - the vice president

31. If both the president and the vice president can no longer serve, who becomes president?
   - the Speaker of the House

32. Who is the Commander–in–Chief of the military?
   - the president

33. Who signs bills to become laws?
   - the president

34. Who vetoes bills?
   - the president

35. What does the president's Cabinet do?
   - advises the president

36. What are two Cabinet–level positions?
   - Secretary of Agriculture
   - Secretary of Commerce
   - Secretary of Defense
   - Secretary of Education
   - Secretary of Energy
   - Secretary of Health and Human Services
   - Secretary of Homeland Security
   - Secretary of Housing and Urban Development
   - Secretary of Interior
   - Secretary of State
   - Secretary of Transportation
   - Secretary of Treasury
   - Secretary of Veterans' Affairs
   - Secretary of Labor
   - Attorney General

37. What does the judicial branch do?
    - reviews laws
    - explains laws
    - resolves disputes (disagreements)
    - decides if a law goes against the Constitution

38. What is the highest court in the United States?
    - the Supreme Court

39. How many justices are on the Supreme Court?
    - nine (9)

40. Who is the Chief Justice of the United States?
    - John Roberts (John G. Roberts, Jr.)

41. Under our Constitution, some powers belong to the federal government. What is one power of the federal government?
    - to print money
    - to declare war
    - to create an army
    - to make treaties

42. Under our Constitution, some powers belong to the states. What is one power of the states?
    - provide schooling and education
    - provide protection (police)
    - provide safety (fire departments)
    - give a driver's license
    - give a marriage license
    - approve zoning and land use

43. Who is the governor of your state?
    - Answers will vary.

44. What is the capital of your state?*
    - Answers will vary.

45. What are the two major political parties in the United States?*
    - Democratic and Republican

46. What is the political party of the president now?
    - Democratic (Party)

47. What is the name of the Speaker of the House of Representatives now?
- (Nancy) Pelosi

C: Rights and Responsibilities

48. There are four amendments to the Constitution about who can vote. Describe <u>one</u> of them.
- Citizens eighteen (18) and older (can vote).
- You don't have to pay (a poll tax) to vote.
- Any citizen can vote. (Women and men can vote.)
- A male citizen of any race (can vote).

49. What is <u>one</u> responsibility that is only for United States citizens?*
- serve on a jury
- vote

50. What are <u>two</u> rights only for United States citizens?
- apply for a federal job
- vote
- run for office
- carry a U.S. passport

51. What are <u>two</u> rights of everyone living in the United States?
- freedom of expression
- freedom of speech
- freedom of assembly
- freedom to petition the government
- freedom of worship
- the right to bear arms *(or the right to have guns)*

52. What do we show loyalty to when we say the Pledge of Allegiance?
- the United States
- the flag

53. What is <u>one</u> promise you make when you become a United States citizen?
- give up loyalty to other countries
- defend the Constitution and laws of the United States
- obey the laws of the United States
- serve in the U.S. military (if needed)
- serve (do important work for) the nation (if needed)
- be loyal to the United States

54. How old do citizens have to be to vote for president?*
   - eighteen (18) and older

55. What are <u>two</u> ways that Americans can participate in their democracy?
   - vote
   - join a political party
   - help with a campaign
   - join a civic group
   - join a community group
   - give an elected official your opinion on an issue
   - call Senators and Representatives
   - publicly support or oppose an issue or policy
   - run for office
   - write to a newspaper

56. When is the last day you can send in federal income tax forms?*
   - April 15

57. When must all men register for the Selective Service?
   - at age eighteen (18)
   - between eighteen (18) and twenty–six (26)

AMERICAN HISTORY

A: Colonial Period and Independence

58. What is <u>one</u> reason colonists came to America?
   - freedom
   - political liberty
   - religious freedom
   - economic opportunity
   - practice their religion
   - escape persecution

59. Who lived in America before the Europeans arrived?
   - Native Americans
   - American Indians

60. What group of people was taken to America and sold as slaves?
   - Africans
   - people from Africa

61. Why did the colonists fight the British?
    - because of high taxes (taxation without representation)
    - because the British army stayed in their houses (boarding, quartering)
    - because they didn't have self–government

62. Who wrote the Declaration of Independence?
    - (Thomas) Jefferson

63. When was the Declaration of Independence adopted?
    - July 4, 1776

64. There were 13 original states. Name <u>three</u>.

• New Hampshire	• Massachusetts
• Rhode Island	• Connecticut
• New York	• New Jersey
• Pennsylvania	• Delaware
• Maryland	• Virginia
• North Carolina	• South Carolina
• Georgia	

65. What happened at the Constitutional Convention?
    - The Constitution was written.
    - The Founding Fathers wrote the Constitution.

66. When was the Constitution written?
    - 1787

67. The Federalist Papers supported the passage of the U.S. Constitution. Name <u>one</u> of the writers.
    - (James) Madison
    - (Alexander) Hamilton
    - (John) Jay

68. What is <u>one</u> thing Benjamin Franklin is famous for?
    - U.S. diplomat
    - oldest member of the Constitutional Convention
    - first Postmaster General of the United States
    - writer of "Poor Richard's Almanac"
    - started the first free libraries

69. Who is the "Father of Our Country"?
- (George) Washington

70. Who was the first president?*
- (George) Washington

B: 1800s

71. What territory did the United States buy from France in 1803?
- the Louisiana Territory
- Louisiana

72. Name <u>one</u> war fought by the United States in the 1800s.
- War of 1812
- Mexican–American War
- Civil War
- Spanish–American War

73. Name the U.S. war between the North and the South.
- the Civil War
- the War between the States

74. Name <u>one</u> problem that led to the Civil War.
- slavery
- economic reasons
- states' rights

75. What was <u>one</u> important thing that Abraham Lincoln did?*
- freed the slaves (Emancipation Proclamation)
- saved (or preserved) the Union
- led the United States during the Civil War

76. What did the Emancipation Proclamation do?
- freed the slaves
- freed slaves in the Confederacy
- freed slaves in the Confederate states
- freed slaves in most Southern states

77. What did Susan B. Anthony do?
- fought for women's rights
- fought for civil rights

C: Recent American History & Other Important Historical Information

78. Name <u>one</u> war fought by the United States in the 1900s.*
- World War I
- World War II
- Korean War
- Vietnam War
- (Persian) Gulf War

79. Who was president during World War I?
- (Woodrow) Wilson

80. Who was president during the Great Depression and World War II?
- (Franklin) Roosevelt

81. Who did the United States fight in World War II?
- Japan, Germany, and Italy

82. Before he was president, Eisenhower was a general. What war was he in?
- World War II

83. During the Cold War, what was the main concern of the United States?
- Communism

84. What movement tried to end racial discrimination?
- civil rights (movement)

85. What did Martin Luther King, Jr. do?*
- fought for civil rights
- worked for equality for all Americans

86. What major event happened on September 11, 2001 in the United States?
- Terrorists attacked the United States.

87. Name <u>one</u> American Indian tribe in the United States.
- Cherokee
- Chippewa
- Apache
- Blackfeet
- Arawak
- Hopi
- Navajo
- Choctaw
- Iroquois
- Seminole
- Shawnee
- Inuit
- Sioux
- Pueblo
- Creek
- Cheyenne
- Mohegan
- Huron
- Oneida
- Lakota
- Crow
- Teton

INTEGRATED CIVICS

A: Geography

88. Name <u>one</u> of the two longest rivers in the United States.
- Missouri (River)
- Mississippi (River)

89. What ocean is on the West Coast of the United States?
- Pacific (Ocean)

90. What ocean is on the East Coast of the United States?
- Atlantic (Ocean)

91. Name <u>one</u> U.S. territory.
- Puerto Rico
- U.S. Virgin Islands
- American Samoa
- Northern Mariana Islands
- Guam

92. Name <u>one</u> state that borders Canada.
- Maine
- New York
- Michigan
- Montana
- Alaska
- New Hampshire
- Pennsylvania
- Minnesota
- Idaho
- Vermont
- Ohio
- North Dakota
- Washington

93. Name <u>one</u> state that borders Mexico.
- California
- Arizona
- New Mexico
- Texas

94. What is the capital of the United States?*
- Washington, D.C.

95. Where is the Statue of Liberty?*
- New York (Harbor)
- Liberty Island
[Also acceptable are New Jersey, near New York City, and on the Hudson (River).]

B. Symbols

96. Why does the flag have 13 stripes?
  - because there were 13 original colonies
  - because the stripes represent the original colonies

97. Why does the flag have 50 stars?*
  - because there is one star for each state
  - because each star represents a state
  - because there are 50 states

98. What is the name of the national anthem?
  - The Star–Spangled Banner

C: Holidays

99. When do we celebrate Independence Day?*
  - July 4

100. Name <u>two</u> national U.S. holidays.
  - New Year's Day
  - Martin Luther King, Jr., Day
  - Presidents' Day
  - Memorial Day
  - Independence Day
  - Labor Day
  - Columbus Day
  - Veterans Day
  - Thanksgiving
  - Christmas